«VOI AC-DMS»

IT-Compliance and Information Security

Audit criteria
for electronic document
management processes
and associated IT solutions

Completely revised 5th edition

Audit criteria for electronic document management processes and associated IT solutions

A joint publication of VOI e.V. with the kind cooperation of TÜV Informationstechnik GmbH, TÜV NORD GROUP.

Published by
VOI – voice of information
Verband Organisations- und Informationssysteme e.V.
Heilsbachstraße 25, 53123 Bonn Tel.: +49.228.908.2090 Fax: +49.228.908.2091
E-Mail: voi@voi.de Internet: http://www.voi.de

Edition: 5th revised edition, 2019

Editorial Manager: Ralf Kaspras

Collaborators in the 5th edition (2019):
Alexander D. Balzer, Dr. Klaus-Peter Elpel, Volker Feist, Wilhelm Flintrop, Axel Janhoff, Ralf Kaspras, Lothar Leger, Peter J. Schmerler, Jan Prochnow, Jörg Rogalla (all VOI e.V.); Dr. Christoph Sutter (TÜViT, TÜV NORD GROUP)

Collaborators in earlier editions:
Thorsten Brand, Dr. Gunther Ernst, Joachim Faulhaber, Christian Friedrichs, Sven Gust, Wolfgang Heinrich, Dr. Knuth Lange, Volker Langer, Andreas Liebling, Peter Manias, Christian Mosler, Jens Müller, Daniel Pelke, Carsten Pohlmann, Karl-Heinz Reiß, Volker von Kannen-Steinert, Berthold Weghaus, Dieter Weinle, Bernhard Zöller

Review:
Alexander D. Balzer, Axel Janhoff, Dr, Klaus-Peter Elpel, Peter Schmerler, Ralf Kaspras

Picture credits for ICONs: © kanate – fotolia.com
Graphics: © VOI e.V. Updated by Peter J. Schmerler
Cover design & book layout: Ingeborg Helzle Grafikdesign Köln
Production: BoD – Books on Demand, Norderstedt

Translated from German: Elizabeth Flint (Newcastle, GB)

ISBN 978-3-932898-28-0

Contents

1. Foreword of VOI

Since 2000, the VOI AC-DMS has stood for compliance in the "digitisation of formerly paper-based processes" and the "design of digital processes", with a major focus on legally compliant and auditable capture, generation, processing, use, reproduction and storage of digital documents of all kinds. From the very beginning, not only the document itself was considered, but also the ways and means for achieving "legally compliant and auditable documentation of processes". The overriding goal was and is to be able to demonstrate compliance with laws, contracts, standards and other framework conditions.

Already in the 4th edition, the growing challenge of networking was taken into account, alongside the need to make comprehensive use of value creation potentials from available information and data. These underlying trends have become even more apparent and the shift in emphasis – away from an approach based on application solutions towards consideration of process solutions – has been continued.

Therefore in this new edition, the editorial team has decided to speak of the „solution" and the „IT system" throughout, in order to focus more on the necessary framework and functionalities for handling and using documents, along with their content, and the nature of the process involved in documentation. Further explanations can be found in the "What's new?" section.

Whilst the 4th edition already focused on topics such as big-data and increasing IT risks, the range of the subject and pressure to act have now increased once again. The amount of data theft and the number of attacks on public IT facilities, digital manipulation of elections across national borders, and much more, are visible testimonies to this. However not all issues are so obvious, although many are equally significant. There is, for example, the emerging use of artificial intelligence (AI): who is here the master of "the data" and "the way" in which it is used? Or the use of blockchain technology, where deletion of individual data is not possible! These topics are at the forefront of data protection, which has been massively tightened up in Europe by the new EU General Data Protection Regulation 2016/679 (GDPR) and where severe sanctions now apply.

In the face of challenges precisely such as these, the present guideline offers a method that helps to provide certainty in decisionmaking by systematically analysing cause-and-effect relationships, revealing their true nature and allowing them to be resiliently verified.

One of the main elements that has become increasingly important for demonstrating compliance in the context of information security is the implementation and maintenance of "appropriate process documentation". What is meant by this can be found in the new chapter "Process Documentation".

In addition to its goal of providing guidance for IT compliance in the above context, this document also includes a concept for robust verification and certification. An audit framework geared towards achieving this is therefore also included here. The auditing organisations involved, TÜViT (TÜV NORD GROUP) and VOI-Cert, have designed the auditing method in such a way that the scope for variations in interpretation is kept to a minimum. In the present edition, the range of application has also been extended once again to cover sub-areas – such as procedural documentation, employee qualifications and compliance-relevant IT characteristics – in addition to DMS solutions and DMS systems. Possible interaction with ISO standards such as ISO 19600 "Compliance management systems – Guidelines" and ISO 27001/27002 "Information security management systems" is also taken into account in order to avoid duplication and unnecessary time and effort.

Therefore with this 5th edition of VOI AC-DMS, in particular a strategic further development is taking place, which has affected both the scope of use and the title of the document in equal measure. At the same time, compatibility with the previous version is ensured.

The focus on independence from specific jurisdictions, and on economic viability and best practice, also remains unchanged.

In summary, the VOI AC-DMS provides a practical framework which allows organisations and companies of all sizes to implement IT compliance requirements.

On behalf of the entire editorial team, I wish all our readers success in using this guideline to further develop their IT compliance activities successfully, efficiently and in a way that is fit for the future. To this end, the work is available as the familiar paper edition – and from now on, can also be accessed as an eBook version.

My warmest thanks go to all the contributors who have worked so hard to make this 5th edition possible!

Dipl.-Inform. Ralf Kaspras
Leader of the AC-DMS working group of VOI e.V.

2. Foreword of TÜViT

The digital transformation in the economy continues to accelerate. In many areas, this is leading to a rapid increase in the variety of electronic information and documents in circulation. These must be processed securely and stored in auditable electronic archives.

Two examples of more recent legal standards in this area are the EU General Data Protection Regulation 2016/679 (GDPR) and the eIDAS Regulation 910/2014. The GDPR requires the protection of personal data and contains regulations for secure transmission (with free movement of data). The eIDAS Regulation defines requirements for legally compliant electronic transactions. It thus creates a legal framework for electronic signatures, seals, time stamps, documents, registered mail and their storage.

Both standards contain rules for the verification of implemented security measures by neutral third parties and underline the importance of independent certification. The GDPR specifies voluntary certification. This is intended to confirm that all the relevant protection requirements are met during data processing. In the case of the eIDAS Regulation, conformity assessment is even a prerequisite for legal effects such as equivalence to the signature, integrity of the data and correct indication of origin.

In addition to the principles for the proper keeping and storage of books, records and documents in electronic form and for data access (GoBD) issued by the Federal Ministry of Finance, both legal standards have implications for auditable archiving. For this reason, they have been taken into account in this revised edition of the audit criteria for document management solutions (AC-DMS). The core criteria of orderliness, completeness, traceability, immutability and availability, which have been included in the

AC-DMS since the beginning, remain unchanged. They have thus formed a proven audit basis for around 20 years.

With this revised edition of the AC-DMS, a reliable and up-to-date basis for auditable electronic archiving solutions has been created that points the way to the future.

Dr. Christoph Sutter
Head of the Certification Body TÜV Informationstechnik GmbH
TÜV NORD GROUP

3. What's new?

One vital aspect in the maintenance and updating of the AC-DMS audit criteria is to ensure "process reliability in the long term" – in other words, the ability to update in such a way that the structure, methodology and audit criteria themselves are largely retained and there is only a need for supplementation. In particular, this is intended to ensure that the time and effort required to adapt existing measures based on the AC-DMS audit criteria is limited as far as possible to the new features.

Increased networking and associated division of functions for the handling of digital documents and documentation (record keeping) were already taken into account in the 4th edition of the AC-DMS. Consideration of management and archiving led to awareness of complex overall contexts, expressed in terms of enterprise content management and enterprise information management. Time has not stood still since then, and a number of new technology trends, options and specifications must now also be taken into account. These include topics such as data protection (e.g., the EU-wide DSGVO, 2016/679), eIDAS, blockchain and big-data. Overall, we are moving further away from considering pure application solutions and towards the challenge of having to look at generic processes and being able to reliably evaluate them in terms of compliance.

In order to consistently advance the AC-DMS audit criteria in this direction, the first step was to change the terminology. Until the 4th edition, the terms "document management solution" and "document management system" were still used to describe the technical approach to document handling. From the point of view of the editorial team today, these terms no longer do sufficient justice to the situation, because they narrow down the perspective where it is now necessary to widen it. However, this does not mean that the terms document management solution and document management system no longer have any justification. They remain at the heart of compliance when it comes to dealing with documents and documentation.

Nevertheless, the broader view requires greater emphasis on the documenting of processes per se and thus involves every IT technology and method and every solution that uses IT.

In order to meet these needs, new content has been added and existing content revised. An overview of the most important modifications can be seen below.

New:

- Chapter on "Creation of process documentation on the basis of the audit criteria"
- Audit criterion "Cloud management"

Terms that have been replaced:

- Data carrier → *New:* Storage media
- IT security → *New:* Information security
- Security concept → *New:* Information security concept
- Document Management System
  → *New:* IT system/IT document management system
- Document Management Solution → *New:* Solution

Revised:

- Section regarding "The 10 key guidelines of VOI for compliant electronic archiving"
- Titles of audit criteria or audit criteria themselves, in so far as this became necessary due to replacement of terms or new knowledge and understanding gained

- Explanatory texts and examples regarding audit criteria
- In the Annex, assignment of audit criteria to ISO 9000 has been replaced by ISO 27001.

Note on the replacement of the assignment examples for ISO 9000 to examples for ISO 27001:

The reason for the change is the major relevance of ISO/IEC 27001 within the area of information security.

Note on the section regarding "Creation of process documentation based on audit criteria"

Here, guidelines for creation of consistent process documentation are set out which can be used as a basis for implementation of the requirements for specific documents – for example within the framework of the German GoBD principles for electronic document storage or the documentation and continuity requirements of ISO 27001.

A   AC-DMS Audit criteria

4. Introduction

In order to prove that digital document processes comply with legal and industry-specific requirements, it is necessary to implement legally compliant and auditable recordkeeping. This guideline serves this requirement by demonstrating a suitable procedure (method) for achieving this compliance, along with the possibility of validation (audit criteria).

Special emphasis is placed on the handling and storage of physical and digital documents. At the core is the question of whether digitally managed documents can provide the same level of reliable evidence as „good old paper".

Assessments according to the requirements in this document are based on the following core criteria for document handling: orderliness, completeness, immutability, availability and traceability. Legal compliance and auditability result from coherent and logical interaction between technology and organisation in the individual case.

The foundation for such reliable evidence is provided by process documentation based on the evaluation and assessment criteria described below. If required, proof of legal certainty and auditability can be additionally secured and documented by means of a formal audit and certification by an authorized certification body.

Companies and organisations should see the creation and maintenance of process documentation as an opportunity, as besides fulfilling legal requirements, it leads to a number of organisational benefits. The approach outlined in these guidelines is designed in such a way that it can be applied to the regulatory requirements of any size of company or organisation.

4.1. Technical starting point

In order that electronic documents and data can fulfil a role which is legally binding and has the same status as paper documents, framework conditions must be created which take the particular features of digital form into consideration.

The framework conditions always consist of a carefully harmonised interaction between technical and organisational measures.

On the *technical* side, procedures and systems are needed which provide special functions, and which on the one hand make it possible to handle electronic documents in a suitable fashion, and on the other hand ensure implementation of auditable and secure processes. Functions for auditability particularly include traceability of:

- recording, generation and processing
- storage
- change
- access
- reproduction

Functions for security particularly include the following:

- ensuring the integrity and authenticity of documents, data and protocols
- suitable access protection for data and systems
- the possibility of logging all accesses and processes
- prevention of manipulation and
- prevention of loss and destruction

The *organisational* side includes all actions and measures which safeguard the operation of the solution in a suitable way and guarantee observance of legal and other rules and regulations. These are in particular:

- defined operational and control processes
- a logical and consistent Internal Control System, and
- process documentation.

4.2. Definitions/Boundaries

4.2.1. Document

A document in the context used here basically embodies the meaning of the word "document" as explained in the German reference work known as "Duden". According to this source, a document – based on the Latin origin "documentum" = piece of writing acting as evidence – is an object which is useful in order to provide understanding or explanation.

A "document in the traditional sense" is always bound to a physical information carrier (e.g. paper, stone tablets) and takes from this its characteristics as reliable evidence in relation to origin, time of creation, identity and authenticity.

Typical documents in this sense include contracts, invoices, notes, certificates, deeds, etc.

4.2.2. Electronic document

An "electronic document" is a file which can be generated, stored, displayed and deleted within the framework of a solution. It includes all possible types of files which can be created from any combination of multimedia digital components.

An *electronic* document is created by means of binary coding and is a virtual object, which is therefore devoid of all physical properties providing the character of evidence. The necessary characteristics of evidence must first be created by different means (e.g. electronic signatures, immutable storage).

Note: In this entire publication, the term "document" is used as the generic term and overall concept and therefore includes the concept of "electronic document". The term "electronic document" is only used when this is necessary for differentiation purposes.

4.2.3. IT system

An "IT system" contains the technical components within a concrete and specific solution scenario.

IT components are part of an IT system.

4.2.4. Solution

The new concept of "solution" is at the centre of the system of audit criteria. For achievement of a specific objective, it is defined as a systematic interaction between IT systems and IT components, supported by organisational measures which have to be specifically worked out and formulated for the respective organisation.

The focus is on legal certainty and auditability of the lifecycle of physical and electronic documents. Solutions always have their own individual character, which has to be described.

4.2.5. Solution operator

Those with legal responsibility are understood to be the "solution operators".

For example, if the application operations are outsourced to third parties (e.g. data centres), the legal operator does not change. This means that the operator of a solution is always legally responsible, even in the case of outsourcing.

4.2.6. Proof capability of the solution

A system has "proof capability" if evidence can be provided that all documents within it are capable of being correctly recorded, stored, processed, displayed and deleted. In this connection it must be ensured, for example, that manipulations are prevented and events can be sufficiently traced.

During transformation from the physical to the digital world, characteristics which are used as a basis for determining validity as evidence and framework conditions change. This is shown in the following diagram.

Validity as evidence

Physical world	Digital world
Objects possess physical characteristics	Objects do not possess physical characteristics
Difficult to manipulate	Easy to manipulate
Legal system is in harmony with the situation regarding validity as evidence	Validity as evidence is often unclear, leading to an uncertain legal situation

Figure 1 – Change in the situation regarding validity as evidence

The clear loss of validity as evidence in the digital world must be compensated through the use of suitable means and methods, and new means of demonstrating validity must be created. In this connection it should be noted that the necessary measures result from the context of legislation, economic value and proportionality.

The quality of evidence provided by electronic documents can be improved among other things by means of the following scheme.

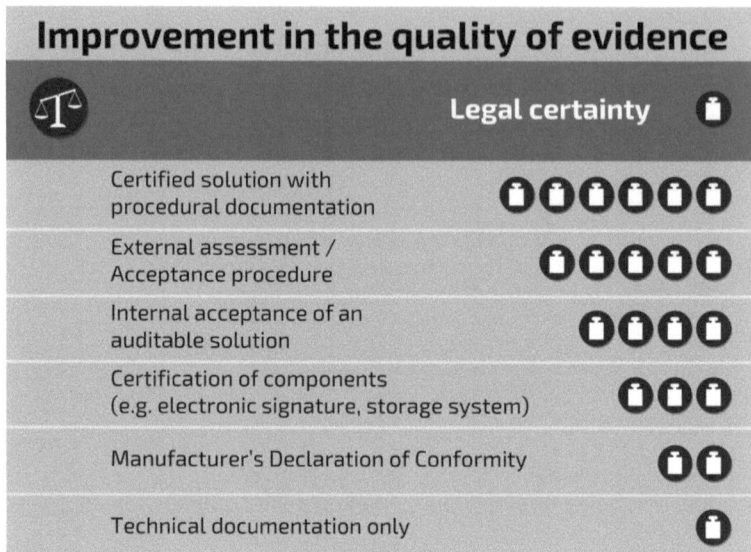

Improvement in the quality of evidence	
	Legal certainty
Certified solution with procedural documentation	⚫⚫⚫⚫⚫⚫
External assessment / Acceptance procedure	⚫⚫⚫⚫⚫
Internal acceptance of an auditable solution	⚫⚫⚫⚫
Certification of components (e.g. electronic signature, storage system)	⚫⚫⚫
Manufacturer's Declaration of Conformity	⚫⚫
Technical documentation only	⚫

Figure 2 – Improvement in the quality of evidence

4.2.7. Legal certainty and auditability

The combined term "legal certainty and auditability" originates from the beginning of the 1990s and stands for correct interaction of framework conditions that have to be applied (targets, legislation, regulations, etc.) and the resultant use of technology and organisation in a concrete validatable form.

4.2.8. The 10 key guidelines of VOI for compliant storage of electronic documents

The first version of the key guidelines of VOI regarding auditable electronic archiving was already drawn up in the 1990s and adapted to further developments in the area of IT over th years. In this new edition, the concept of archiving has been replaced by the concept of storage in the title of this section in order to take account of increasing cloud computing and more stringent requirements for IT compliance. If the term "archive" or "archiving" is used in the following text, it is used in the entire document for reasons of compatibility. Storage of compliance-relevant digital documents and different versions of these must always be legally compliant and auditable.

The guidelines define the requirements for orderliness when implementing an electronic document storage solution and are closely linked to data protection legislation, IT compliance and to standards relevant to auditable storage.

They therefore create the general framework of the requirements which have to be interpreted and described in detail in order to create a concrete and specific technical solution.

1. **Each document must be correctly stored in accordance with the legal requirements and the internal requirements of the organisation.**

   This principle describes the central objective of electronic storage: reliable and legally secure and compliant storage of documents in a regulated fashion. It emphasises that the concrete form of a digital solution is always also dependent on the specific requirements of the particular environment where it is to be used and the associated organisational processes and IT-related implementation. These requirements result from legislative and other legally binding rules and regulations, as well as from the rules that the organisation has set for itself. Organisations which are active internationally have to take into account that the legislative and further binding rules and regulations can differ in some aspects between countries.

2. **The storage must be complete – no document may be lost on its way into the electronic archive or in the archive itself.**

   This principle is based on the fact that all documents that are needed must be recorded and saved in the archive in their entirety. Only in this way is it possible to fulfil legal documentation requirements and ensure gap-free traceability of procedures, events and processes at a later date.

3. **Each document must be archived at the earliest point in time that is possible from the organisational point of view.**
Processing and electronic storage have to take place very soon after the event. A digital solution ensures the integrity and availability of the documents at all times. In so far as immutability of documents is required – also over the long term – this requirement can be fulfilled by the electronic archive at an early stage.

4. **Each document must agree with the original and be archived so as to be immutable.**
This principle reflects the requirement that an archived document must correspond to the original at each point in time in a way that is capable of acting as proof – also over the long term. Depending on the type and purpose of the document, this can mean that the content is identical or that there is also congruence in appearance between the electronically archived version and the original paper or electronic document.

5. **Every document may only be viewed by suitably authorised users.**
This principle serves to protect confidential information and to comply with the rules concerning protection of personal data. A suitable authorisation concept must be developed for and implemented in the solution for this purpose.

6. **Every document must be capable of being searched and displayed within an appropriate time.**
This principle aims at making archived documents available on screen within an appropriate time. The users within the organisation state the maximum tolerable time for search and reproduction based on their own particular requirements. The possibilities here particularly depend on the level of information technology available in the organisation. Studies and experience show that users accept a maximum three-second time lag between the search command and the appearance of the document on the screen.

7. **Unauthorised and/or untraceable deletion of documents shall be excluded from both the technical and organisational points of view and must be organised in such a way that both set archiving periods are adhered to and legal requirements for deletion can be met.**
A document may only be deleted at the earliest at the end of the set archiving period, or it must be deleted immediately if so stipulated by legal requirements – i.e. it must be deleted from the archive.
For example, according to Article 17 of the EU Data Protection Regulation (GDPR), in certain cases a customer has the right to demand immediate deletion of his documents from the electronic archive. The organisation must ensure fulfilment of this demand if the conditions stated in Article 17 are fulfilled, and must inform the customer of the deletion.

8. **Each action in the electronic archiving system which gives rise to a change must be traceably and understandably recorded for those authorised to know.**

   This key guideline is equivalent to the "prohibition of erasure" in bookkeeping. It requires that subsequent changes can be recognised and that the original version of the document can be called up and displayed during the entire storage period.

9. **It must be ensured that the entire organisational and technical process for archiving can be evaluated at any time by an expert third party.**

   This principle aims at providing proof that the archiving solution is in fact in use by the respective operator in the sense of all these principles. In order to provide this proof, on the one hand process documentation is essential, and on the other hand it must always be possible to examine and audit operation in progress in order to establish that it is correct and fit for purpose (e.g. based on system logs and measures within an "Internal Control System" – ICS).

10. **In all migrations and changes to the archiving system, it must be ensured that all the above principles are adhered to.**

    This principle results from the experience that the innovation cycles of the hard- and software used in the archive system are generally a great deal shorter than the set archiving periods of the documents themselves (e.g. mortgage contracts).
    Therefore, during the storage period there are practically always changes to the archive system (from replacement of individual items of equipment up to migration of the complete archive into a completely different technical system). All the above principles must be obeyed when such migration meas-

ures take place. In particular, changes and migration measures must be carefully documented, so that their correctness and orderliness can be checked during the entire archiving period of the migrated documents.

4.2.9. Process documentation as a basic regulatory requirement

In relation to the AC-DMS, the process documentation provides the foundation for proof of "legal certainty and auditability" and therefore for confirmation of the quality and performance statements associated with the procedures described.

Within this frame of reference it describes, starting from the specific task, components, ways of functioning and interaction of organisation and technology in a logical, complete form which is capable of verification.

In addition, the process documentation has to describe changes in processes near to the event and in chronological order without any gaps. In other words, the process documentation itself is subject to an ongoing process which can be traced in terms of its content (versioning and version management).

The method which monitors and assures the legal certainty and auditability of a process documented in this way – and also of the process documentation itself – is described in the chapter concerned with the "Internal Control System (ICS)".

4.2.10. Objects of inspection and testing

In this connection, the objects of inspection and testing (audit) are as follows:

- the process documentation
- the concrete solution

4.2.11. Gender-specific use of language

Gender-specific forms of language are not used to express an otherwise identical concept. All speech related to persons relates to all genders equally.

5. Methodology of the AC-DMS

5.1. Definition of core criteria

A solution is assessed on the basis of the following core criteria:

- orderliness
- completeness
- traceability
- immutability
- availability

Each individual evaluation criterion (as described in Chapter 7) is assessed on this basis. The core criteria are therefore to be understood as checkpoints within each individual evaluation criterion.

5.1.1. Orderliness

Several partial aspects which serve for fulfilment of the legal framework conditions are brought together under the core criterion of "orderliness". These aspects encompass legal, governmental, official and internal rules and regulations and also contractual obligations. They include among others:

- ensuring order within the system, so that the documents and data are unambiguously indexed. This also involves correct time-related and subject-related assignment of the documents – for example to a booking period or a project
- ensuring timely processing of the documents and data in order to exclude possible losses and manipulations prior to archiving

- ensuring correctness through congruence of the original and archived document in accordance with the requirements – for example identical nature of images, contents, colour and fulfilment of signature requirements
- ensuring confidentiality, so that documents and data can only be viewed and processed by authorised users
- clear definition of responsibilities, both internal responsibilities and those related to outsourcing installation of an "Internal Control System" (ICS)

5.1.2. Completeness

The core criterion of "completeness" of a solution is understood to mean ensuring gap-free recording and storage of all relevant data and documents up to their loss-free reproduction over the entire period during which the documents have to be retained.

5.1.3. Immutability

The core criterion of "immutability" ensures that no more changes can be made to documents and data. If changes are essential (e.g. double archiving runs, correction of false indexing), it is possible to make changes, but the original state and the time sequence and effect of changes must be capable of tracking and understanding at all times.

Immutability must be ensured by means of both technical and organisational measures and, in addition to the archived documents themselves, also affects the access information (metadata/index values), electronic signatures and all components which support proof and evidence capability, such as the process documentation and system and test protocols. The time from which the immutability should apply must also be clearly laid down in the life cycle of the documents.

5.1.4. Availability

The core criterion of "availability" ensures that the documents and data can be read and processed according to the requirements at all times. This includes, for example, adherence to the required access times, physical security measures, data backup and transfer to third-party locations and arrangements for maintenance, standard and emergency operation as well as a migration concept.

5.1.5. Traceability

The core criterion of "traceability" requires that a third party versed in the art must be able to gain an overview of the existing solution along with its processes within an appropriate period of time, and use and the test and release procedures used in relation to it.

On the one hand this relates to the entire system, including all processes which have to be documented within the framework of a set of process documentation. On the other hand, it must be possible to understand specialised and operative processes, whereby the depth and extent of recording is dependent on the intended use. Logs which make certain operations traceable are required for this purpose. Examples of such operations are invoice release, contract approval, index change, document deletion and user administration.

5.2. Creation of process documentation based on audit criteria

AC-DMS evaluation areas (as described in Chapter 6) are designed in such a way that demarcation between control and audit issues is already assured by their structure. However, application-related, individual control and audit requirements are not covered by this and require further design measures. The role of the process documentation must be precisely defined in the specific application case. Legally compliant and auditable process documentation always describes a specific individual use case.

In the context of existing IT compliance requirements and further verification requirements, for example vis-à-vis supervisory authorities, strategically well-designed process documentation can avoid duplication of work, reduce complexity, and therefore provide legal certainty and auditability in an effective and efficient way.

If process documentation in general is to be resilient in the area of IT compliance and in particular in the areas of Legal certainty and auditability, in addition to strategic orientation, technical and organisational design is of the utmost importance. This includes the following features in particular:

- ongoing and timely updating and maintenance of internal consistency
- chronologically gap-free traceability for the whole period when verification requirements apply – this includes appropriate version management at a sufficiently defined and justified level of detail

The core criteria of orderliness, completeness, immutability, availability and traceability are also the relevant key parameters for process documentation. Efficient process documentation incorporates all quality and compliance assurance measures. It is the central tool for compliance management of IT solutions.

It is also important to clarify the question of the appropriate depth of description. On this point in particular, it is advisable to ascertain the normal practice for the specific application and to have this confirmed by suitable experts and assessment organisations. The possible risks of damage must be taken as a basis and considered for the proportionality of the documentation.

Compliance-oriented process documentation shows that processes are designed systematically and responsibly, taking into account the relevant situation.

As an essential component of IT compliance, the management of process documentation belongs to the area of responsibility of top management.

5.3. Separation of areas of application

Document processes extend through all areas of an organisation. Use of a solution therefore often extends over areas that have different legal implications and requirements. These areas must therefore be presented clearly and provided with boundaries, in order that their correctness can be examined early within their context.

The following diagram shows an example of the use of a solution over various areas of application (bookkeeping, personnel files, etc.). It also makes clear how on the one hand content-related facts have to be divided up and on the other hand how these must be clearly differentiated from the technical implementation.

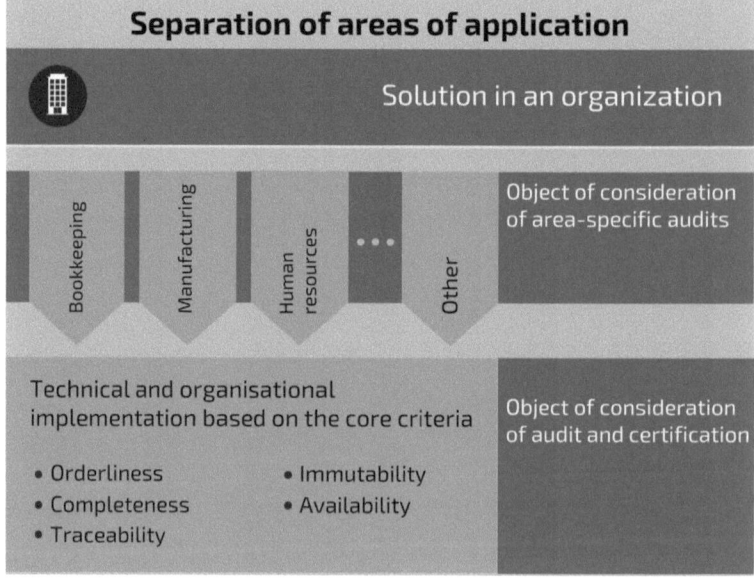

Figure 3 - Separation of areas of application

6. Overview of the evaluation areas

The criteria described in this publication comprise the requirements for certification of a solution.

All individual criteria are formulated as positive statements. The statements are in this sense „K.O. criteria" (criteria which must be fulfilled without fail).

If individual criteria are not considered applicable for the solution, this must be justified in each particular case.

A certification can only take place if all relevant criteria have been established as applicable to the solution to be assessed.

The process documentation on which the audit is based must deal appropriately with all relevant aspects of the solution and therefore allow assessment of compliance with the requirements. This means that it must contain statements regarding the points listed below:

1. General description of the area of use
2. Task-related and inherently logical solution
3. Technical solution
4. Information security
5. Technical operation
6. Long-term availability and migration
7. Employee qualification
8. Testing
9. Outsourcing
10. Description of the Internal Control System (ICS)

More details can be found in the paragraphs describing the requirements for the individual evaluation criteria.

6.1. General description of the area of use

Using the description, an auditor from outside the organisation must be able to gain a general understanding of the organisation, its structural and procedural organisation and also the way in which the solution is integrated into the organisation and its operations.

6.2. Task-related and inherently logical solution

The description shall be structured in such a way that the following items can be understood by an auditor from outside the organisation. The following items are included in the description:

- the structural and procedural organisation of the organisation units
- the individual tasks associated with the solution from the point of view of the user
- the document or data inventories which are relevant for the solution
- the legal framework conditions which are relevant to the solution
- the company-specific requirements for the solution and
- all processes and instructions which are necessary in order to fulfil the objectives of the solution in the sense of the evaluation areas listed above
- all documentation which testifies to proper use for the intended purpose.

6.3. Technical solution

The technical implementation of the solution shall be described in an understandable way. Starting from a general overview, both the individual components of the solution (hardware and software), and also their interaction, are described.

6.4. Information security

An information security concept shall exist in which the possible risks in relation to information security and data protection are named and shown in relation to the respective security measures.

6.5. Technical operation

A description of the measures for assuring orderly and proper operation, and their implementation, shall be provided (operating conditions, prerequisites for operation and operating processes).

6.6. Long-term availability and migration

Long-term availability is the capacity to keep data and documents available and usable over very long periods of time.

Migration capability is one necessary characteristic of solutions, arising from the requirement for long-term availability.

A detailed concept and/or migration documentation must be available of how long-term availability and migration capability are ensured.

6.7. Employee qualification

The qualifications of the internal and external employees which are necessary for the use and orderly operation of the solution shall be described. Corresponding qualification of the relevant employees shall be proven and corresponding measures for achieving the required qualification shall be documented.

6.8. Tests

Fulfilment of the application-specific requirements of the procedures on which the focus is placed and which are described in the process documentation, and also the functionality of the solution, are ensured by means of traceable tests. A corresponding test concept and also corresponding test schedules and protocols must be available.

6.9. Outsourcing

The special feature of outsourcing is that the solution or parts of it are not implemented by the operator himself, but by one or more service providers commissioned by him. This also includes cloud computing, in so far as the service is provided by third parties in the legal sense. Responsibility for adherence to the legal regulations and for fulfilment of core criteria for the outsourced portions of the solution always remains with the operator, in this case acting as customer. Neither is he released from this responsibility by any contractual arrangements with the outsourcing service provider.

Note:

Developments in legal practice and with regard to compliance requirements not only underline this responsibility, but also require regular control and checking of the subcontractor to ensure implementation and ongoing adherence to the requirements.

The parts of the solutions which are outsourced must be described in their entirety, taking this aspect particularly into consideration.

6.10. Description of the Internal Control System (ICS)

The "Internal Control System" (ICS) is the totality of all control measures. It comprises all organisational and technical measures and also unambiguous and complete assignment of responsibilities.

These also include the control measures which are needed in order to guarantee the necessary legal certainty and auditability of the solution. They particularly include management of the process documentation and its ongoing and prompt updating.

The description of the ICS provides a logical description of the methods whereby origin, implementation, updating and continuous monitoring of the control measures are assured.

7. Evaluation criteria

This section contains the concrete audit criteria and also explanations to aid general understanding.

7.1. General description of the area of use

In order that an external auditor can form a picture of the framework conditions of the solution, the area of use must be described in sufficient detail.

In addition to the purpose and reason for the use of the solution, the type of documents (e.g. contracts, invoices, drawings) and scope should be briefly described.

In particular, the laws to be applied, internal rules and guidelines, and the risks to be taken into consideration, are fundamental elements of the description.

7.1.1. Description of the organisation

The company or organisation shall be described in such a way that a clear image of its tasks and objectives is created.

> Explanation
>
> A general description of the activities of the company and its core competencies, including a short description of the corresponding industry sector, is sufficient. The intention is to communicate an impression of the significance of the solution for the company or organisation.

7.1.2. Locations

The precise locations of the organisational units and the IT components shall be described.

> **Explanation**
>
> This should include the precise address(es) of the location(s) and also the names of the divisions or departments sited there, e.g. data centre XY. A description should also be given of which parts of the system are operated at which locations.

7.1.3. Organisation structure

The organisation structure shall be represented in understandable form by means of text and graphics.

> **Explanation**
>
> It must be clear which organisational units are responsible for the following aspects of the solution:
>
> - specific responsibility for the solution
> - administration of users, authentication and access rights
> - target-based and technical further development of the solution
> - support and operation of the solution
> - building-related and technical safety and security of the solution
> - continual updating of the process documentation
>
> The description of the general organisation provides the third-party auditor with the framework for evaluation of individual organisational measures. The depth of the description is based on this objective. The functional departments and organisational units are described and made clear by means of organisation charts.

7.2. Task-related and inherently logical solution

The purpose and task of the solution shall be described from the task-related point of view and also from the point of view of its specific applicability to the specialist departments. The level of detail must be sufficient to explain the concrete form of the installed solution against the background of the particular departmental objectives.

7.2.1. Framework, tasks and guidelines

The framework and the tasks (objectives) of the solution shall be described. All rules which are to be fulfilled by the solution such as laws, ordinances, regulations, conditions, restrictions, agreements and contracts are listed.

Explanation

The solution itself should be described at an understandable technical level. This includes the purpose, processes, locations and work organisation and also the distribution of tasks. The legal requirements under which the system is operated must be clear (e.g. financial accounting: HGB – German Commercial Code, AO – Fiscal Code). There are also regulations and standards which contain concrete rules regarding the operation of IT systems (e.g. Securities Trading Act – German: WpHG) and require specific measures.

For example, the new data protection rules apply (GDPR and the new Federal Data Protection Act – BDSG-neu).

7.2.2. Description of the organisation

A description of the organisation of the relevant areas shall be provided.

The description provides more details with regard to the organisation, but only related to the organisation units affected by the solution. Responsibilities in relation to generation, processing, administration, archiving and destruction of documents should be clearly recognisable. In so far as external organisation units are involved (outsourcing), these should also be described.

7.2.3. Document inventories

A description of the document inventories including the necessary storage periods shall be provided. It must be stated how the storage periods are to be implemented.

Explanation

The inventories are classified from the point of view of quality and the framework volumes are stated. A difference is made between different types of document (e.g. booking slips, invoices, correspondence, technical product documentation). These are described according to type and period of storage. Depending on the application scenario (e.g. with the use of BSI TR-03138 (RESISCAN)) the protection requirements for the information must also be specified.

Relevant (e.g. legal/in-house/organisational) rules and regulations for the handling of the different types of documents must be described. Based on their extremely important role, attention is drawn here to current data protection regulations, which particularly in the context of storage periods may require special rules and mechanisms.

Note: It must be taken into account that in some cases documents have to be stored in their original format (e.g. paper originals, emails, electronic invoices).

7.2.4. Digitisation and taking over of paper documents

The procedure for digitisation, takeover and indexing of paper documents shall be described.

> **Explanation**
>
> Scanning is a multi-stage process which must be secured from the organisational point of view at all stages in order to guarantee complete and correct recording of all documents. This applies equally to the scanning of individual documents and to stack scanning. In any case, the image quality and complete recording of the documents must be checked on a regular basis.

7.2.5. Destruction of paper and other original documents

The destruction of paper and other original documents shall be described, stating the corresponding legal and in-house requirements.

> **Explanation**
>
> Within the context of digitisation of paper documents, there is often also the wish to destroy the paper documents after the digitisation process. If and how this can occur must as a rule be determined according to the particular framework conditions (e.g. requirements of commercial or civil law). Criteria and deadlines for the destruction must be described accordingly. In addition, it must be considered that whatever disturbances occur to the operation of the solution, the documents must still be available in their original form and be capable of being scanned in again until their orderly recording is secure and an archive backup has been created. Prior to destruction it must also be ensured that there is congruence of content/image between the archived docu-

ments and the documents to be destroyed. Paper originals may not be destroyed if legislation or contractual provisions require written form or if it is necessary to provide original documents.

In order to maintain prima facie proof, the paper documents should be transformed into an electronic format according to the state of technology, e.g. in accordance with BSI TR03138 (RESISCAN) or VOI-CERT "TR-RESISCAN ready" and then stored in such a way that auditability is ensured and evidential integrity is retained.

If original documents are stored in addition to the electronic copies, this must either be noted on the electronic documents or clear rules must exist in this regard (for example, defined types of documents).

The same applies to other types of media that are transformed into electronic format, such as for example films or pictures, and to conversion or change of the formats of electronic documents.

7.2.6. Takeover of documents received in electronic form

The procedure for taking over originally digital documents (files) shall be described.

Explanation

Documents received in electronic form must be handled in exactly the same way as digitised documents from the technical point of view. However, besides the original documents, additional data are often also present (e.g. compressed transfer formats, signature information or log files). It must also be considered whether the original file names and attributes have to be retained or if changes to these are possible. A decision must be made as to whether this additional information is also to be stored, and this decision should be documented accordingly.

The description of the takeover process must include among other things early, correct and complete takeover of the documents. Corresponding work instructions must be present and available. The files may only be deleted from the original system after error-free takeover into the solution and subsequent data saving has been carried out.

Documents available in digital form, e.g. files from MS Office applications, are taken over into the solution by means of manual file recording or automatically using other technical methods.

If, for example, it should be necessary to prove within a particular use case that documents/information have not been changed following receipt, these have to be provided with e.g. a signature or a seal before archiving, or secured using another method which assures integrity.

7.2.7. Handling of documents with electronic signatures

Use of electronic signatures, the associated verification procedures and also maintenance of the validity of the signature during the specified archiving period shall be described. The procedure for taking over, verification and retention of the value of electronically signed documents as evidence shall also be described.

Explanation

A difference should be made between incoming signed and sealed documents and signatures and seals generated within the organisation, and also time stamps in the sense of EU Regulation 910/2014 (eIDAS).

It should be taken into account that signature validity is dependent upon the status of the certificate used and the suitability of the algorithms. If the validity expires within the storage/archiving period of the documents, additional measures must be taken in order to maintain evidential integrity. It must therefore be described if and how evidential integrity is maintained in case this becomes necessary and how organisation of the data is regulated in order to make this possible. Procedures according to TR-ESOR (evidentiary value preservation) or eIDAS (electronic identification and trust services for electronic transactions in the single market) can be used here, for example.

The desired/required level of evidentiary provision must always be described.

The process of signature or time stamp generation (individual/mass generation) must be described. In the case of electronic signatures which are received, handling and implementation of verification of the signatures should also be documented if applicable.

Furthermore, the organisational processes for certificate management and administration should be described if applicable (renewal, loss, theft, blocking, etc.).

The electronic signature or electronic seal is lost in the course of a format transformation (e.g. printing, digital change of format) or becomes invalid if appropriate measures are not taken. It must be described how electronic signatures are handled in such cases, e.g. how a transfer note is generated.

7.2.8. Handling of emails

The procedures for takeover and indexing of emails and any documents and annexes/appendices contained in them shall be described, along with the applicable legal and internal requirements.

Explanation

A series of criteria must be taken into consideration in the handling of emails. Creation of a separate guideline for the handling of emails is recommended. The guideline should include the following points:

- decision as to whether only the attachments and/or also the emails themselves are to be kept – in particular, this affects signed and/or encrypted emails
- rules and procedures for examination of signed emails and the decryption of encrypted emails
- prohibition on or acceptance of private emails, and if appropriate rules for handling of private emails
- rules regarding spam and virus filters
- rules for data protection for business and private emails
- rules for classification of business and tax-relevant emails
- rules for the assignment of emails to individual business processes, areas, cases or transactions
- rules for differentiating between emails where there is a duty to archive, emails which are worthy of being archived and those which are not worthy

The following additional criteria must be taken into account for legally compliant and verifiable De-Mail (according to the De-Mail Act) and electronic registered mail according to elDAS (both referred to as "electronic registered mail" in the following text):

- prohibition or permissibility of private electronic registered mails; if appropriate, rules regarding handling of private electronic registered mails
- rules on data protection for business and, if applicable, private electronic registered mails

- rules for classification of business-relevant and tax-relevant electronic registered mails
- rules for allocation of electronic registered mails to individual business processes, areas, cases or transactions
- rules as to who is allowed to use electronic registered mails
- rules for storage of all electronic registered mails and annexes/appendices

In so far as company agreements and employment contracts contain provisions that concern these points, this must be documented.

In the archiving of emails/electronic registered mails, particular attention must be paid to separation of tax-relevant and non-tax-relevant mails. Emails/electronic registered mails with relevance to bookkeeping are "original electronic documents" in the sense of commercial and tax law and are subject to further rules and regulations.

In so far as emails/electronic registered mails with several recipients and/or emails with the same file attachments are saved in the archive in such a way as to save space ("Single Instance"), this must be documented accordingly.

The link between the individual emails/electronic registered mails and the attachments must be clearly shown in the system.

It must be ensured that, by organisational and/or technical means, the emails/electronic registered mails that have to be archived are identified and are transferred into the system in good time, correctly and completely (including their file attachments). The emails/electronic registered mails are only deleted from the email server or client after error-free transfer into the system has been completed.

Individual emails can be transferred through explicit actions of individual users. As an alternative, automatic transfer procedures can transfer emails/electronic registered mails into the system following certain rules, without user action. In addition to the purely technical transfer of emails/electronic registered mails, organisational rules and arrangements are often necessary in connection with archiving.

Note: In this context, email refers to secure (signed and/or encoded) and unsecured emails regardless of the provider. For the use case of secure implementation of the transport of emails, the Federal Office for Information Security has issued the Technical Regulation "BSI TR-03108-1: Secure E-Mail Transport". ISO/IEC 27010 also deals with secure communication between various parties, for example.

7.2.9. Takeover procedure for mass digital data

The procedure for takeover and indexing of mass digital data shall be described.

Explanation

By digital mass data are meant document or print data streams (e.g. COLD) which are generated automatically in large volumes. These must be taken over into the solution correctly and completely within a short period of time. Documents of this kind are frequently generated from outside (third-party) systems, so that among other things specific interface descriptions may be needed. The files may only be deleted in the original system when error-free takeover into the solution, with subsequent data saving, has been completed. In some application scenarios, an IT document management system is operated acting quasi as an extension module of a lead ERP (enterprise resource planning) system, with data exchange performed via a defined interface. Typically, not all functions of the ECM/IT (ECM – enterprise content management) document management system are used in such cases, for example indexing and search are often performed within the ERP system instead of within the ECM/IT document management system. However, the entire recording and processing procedure must be made transparent in the process documentation within the overall context of the solution, whereby reference can be made to the documentation of the lead system if appropriate.

The ECM/IT document management system must provide the functions expected of it by the lead system according to the interface specification.

7.2.10. Indexing

The procedure for indexing shall be described. Work instructions shall be available for manual indexing processes.

Explanation

Clear categorisation criteria are assigned to a document by means of indexing. These are of particular significance for later searching and finding of documents within the solution. Indexing can be performed manually, semi-automatically or fully-automatically.

Particular risks can arise during manual indexing because of incorrect data entry. The description must therefore particularly show how these risks are minimised, for example through suitable design of the human-machine interface and corresponding work instructions for the personnel responsible for the recording.

In the case of automatic indexing, the necessary index values are assigned by the solution. The index values are drawn

directly or indirectly from the documents (e.g. OCR, ICR, assignment via barcodes or takeover of values from external databases).
Correctness must be ensured for both manual and also semi- and fully-automatic indexing by both technical and organisational means (e.g. clarity and unambiguous nature of key values with identifying function, selection lists, checksum processes, recognition of double recording, random sample checks, plausibility checks).

7.2.11. Archiving

The process for immutable archiving of documents shall be described.

Explanation

It must be ensured that document archiving is secure and can be traced and logically understood and that archived documents cannot be changed. This does not exclude the possibility that if necessary, new versions of archived documents can be generated as needed (renditions, revisions); the original version and all subsequent versions must then, however, always be capable of reconstruction. A gap-free document history must therefore always be present. Archiving of documents must be recorded/logged in a suitable fashion. For assessment to establish if archiving is suitable see also "The 10 Key Guidelines of VOI for compliant storage of electronic documents".

7.2.12. Search and access

The procedures for accessing documents shall be described and are based on an agreed authorisation concept.

It must be possible to search for and find each document sufficiently quickly at any time using its index values. The search must fulfil the requirements of the authorisation concept (e.g. no display of unauthorised documents in "found" lists).

Access to documents is based on the authorisations released in the individual case (e.g. only display "found" list, read only, or also process and provide with version number). It must be ensured that the access traceability process fulfils the necessary internal and legal requirements.

In addition, the means that can be used for search and access are described (e.g. IT system/archive client, browser, mobile client).

The access and the search must be secured by technical means against improper use.

7.2.13. Check-in/check-out

The procedure for check-in/check-out of a document shall be described.

If required, a document is blocked by means of a check-out function, so that uncoordinated simultaneous processing is not possible. At the same time, it must be ensured that a checked-out document can be checked in again based on corresponding authorisations.

7.2.14. Editing and assigning versions

The procedure for editing and assigning versions to documents shall be described.

New versions of a document can be generated if required. The changes are recorded so that they can be tracked and understood; this relates both to the document content and also to the index values. It must also be possible to recognise who established what version and when.

For example, annotations can be added to documents archived as images or content can be changed in the case of CI documents (e.g. Word or Excel files). In both cases, new documents and therefore new versions are created alongside the original documents. Old versions can be displayed if required. The document history must be archived without gaps over the entire lifetime of a document.

7.2.15. Onward transfer

The procedure for onward transfer of documents shall be described and compliance with authorisations ensured.

Explanation

Documents can be transferred on if necessary (e.g. for checking of content, fulfilling the "four-eyes" principle, further processing). Documents can be transferred on to persons, organisation units or to automatic processing procedures, e.g. with the help of electronic mailboxes.

Here it must be recorded what organisational measures (e.g. in the form of work instructions) and/or what automatic onward transfer functions (e.g. workflow components, email) are used.

Suitable recording/logging must be ensured.

In the case of information/documents where data protection is relevant, corresponding protection must be provided by means of encryption.

7.2.16. Reproduction

The procedures for the reproduction of a document shall be described.

> **Explanation**
>
> When documents from the IT system are displayed and printed, the required agreement with the original document (paper original or original digital document) must be ensured. Depending on technical or legal requirements, the agreement may relate to content or to reproduction of an image which is true to the original.

7.2.17. Deletion

The procedure for deleting documents shall be described.

> **Explanation**
>
> Deletion is basically not permitted within the context of auditable archiving. Nevertheless there may be the necessity (for example for reasons of data protection) to delete documents or to remove them from the possibility of standard accessing (logical deletion). They can then only be called up with special authorisation.
>
> For example, the GDPR expressly provides for the right of deletion if the purpose of the storage no longer exists. It is also possible to rescind an agreement once given in so far as the requirements stated in the GDPR are fulfilled. Deletion is also intended when the specified storage period ends. Deviations from this are possible if the data processing and/or storage is absolutely necessary in order to fulfil an obligation according to the law of the European Union or its member states.

The obligation of deletion stated in the GDPR is excluded, if the data processing or storage are absolutely necessary for fulfilling an obligation according to the law of the European Union or its members states. This includes, for example, the legally relevant duty of storage according to Article 147 AO (German Tax Law) or Article 157 in association with Article 238 HGB (German Commercial Code).

Particular legal requirements may exist in the individual case where it must be possible to prove that primary data and index values were physically deleted at a particular time. In so far as deleted documents are no longer permitted to be present on backup storage media, the back-up processes must be designed accordingly. In the case of complete physical deletion, it may also be necessary to recopy storage media (omitting the documents to be deleted), and then to physically destroy the original storage media.

Deletion of documents must be recorded in a way which can be tracked and understood. In many cases, it is sufficient to record the deletion of an entire body of documents as a single event. Records of the deletion of each individual document within the body of documents are then no longer necessary.

7.3. Technical solution

The degree of detail in the description of the technical hardware and software components depends on the importance of the individual components for the solution in question. The components which are fundamental to the function and orderliness, such as the archive server, are documented in detail and their suitability in terms of the five core criteria is described. In contrast, in many cases the precise details of the items of equipment used as pure information workstations for document research are not important.

The designations, tasks, interactions and interfaces of the hardware and software components used, as well as the infrastructures, must be documented.

7.3.1. Graphic representation of the system
The technical system solution shall be represented in graphic form.

Explanation

This representation provides a logical and understandable overview of the individual system components and their context within the solution. The objective of this criterion is to achieve overall ease of understanding, in order that the components described can be correctly assigned and assessed.

7.3.2. Storage systems
The storage systems shall be described, in particular with regard to immutability and availability of the recorded documents and data.

It is clear how the storage systems that are used fulfil these requirements independently or dependent on further components.

7.3.3. Recording systems

The recording systems shall be described, particularly with regard to completeness and immutability of the recorded documents and data.

Explanation

Recording systems are, for example, scanners, barcode readers or multifunctional devices in association with e.g. Optical Character Recognition (OCR). It is described how scanners and recognition and recording software work together, how the immutability of the documents is achieved in this phase, and how the transfer to the archive components of the solution is implemented. In addition, it must become clear how completeness and orderliness are guaranteed during the recording process.

A comprehensive recommendation for organisational and technical design of the recording process is available in the form of the Technical Regulation (German: Technische Richtlinie) TR-03138 (RESISCAN) from the Federal Office for Information Security (BSI) on the subject of "replacement scanning". If the final intention is to destroy the paper originals, orientation on TR-03138 is useful.

In so far as electronic documents and data are taken over, the processes used are generally automated to a greater extent. However, these processes must still fulfil the aforementioned criteria (completeness, immutability, etc.).

7.3.4. Output systems

It shall be described that the output systems used are suitable to undertake reproduction in relation to the tasks of the solution.

> Explanation
>
> The standard output devices are monitors and printers. In some cases, specialist output devices are also used for certain areas. When considering the suitability of equipment, the most important aspects are the resolution, representation of colours, or special formats which allow congruence of the content and graphics with the original documents.

7.3.5. Virtualisation

The virtual environment and also the number and type of the virtual machines used shall be described. Assignment of the software to virtual servers, hardware servers and specific locations shall be implemented.

> Explanation
>
> The virtual environment must be described so that the complexity and the know-how that is necessary can be assessed. The description is also important in order to know what resources of what software are being used (for example for risk assessment regarding failures). This means that statements regarding fail-safe measures must be included in the description (such as use of backup systems). These measures should only be mentioned quite briefly here, and then should be described in more detail in the chapter "Information security".

7.3.6. Server hardware

The servers with all their major components shall be described so that it is possible to assign the software to specific servers and specific locations, and assessment of suitability can be carried out.

> **Explanation**
>
> The server components that are relevant for the solution (also within the framework of virtual environments) must be described. In addition to the archive servers, this also includes machines on which databases, communication software, etc. are installed.

7.3.7. Client hardware

The client hardware that is used with all its major components shall be described so that it is possible to assign the software to specific workstations and locations and an assessment of suitability can be carried out.

> **Explanation**
>
> Active client hardware components (e.g. for data recording or indexing) must be described. Passive client hardware components (search/research workstations) need only be detailed to the extent that is necessary in relation to functional and security aspects of the document management task.

7.3.8. Server software

The server software components used with their versions and also their adaptations (customizing) shall be described.

> **Explanation**
>
> This relates on the one hand to basic software such as operating systems, application servers or databases, and on

the other hand to the special solution modules on the server side.

Normally the documentation of the manufacturer is sufficient to describe the functionality of standard software (data sheets, user manuals, etc.). The versions used should be recorded and individual adaptations created by means of customizing should be described.

7.3.9. Client software

The client software components that are used shall be described along with their adaptations (customizing). The user interfaces for input and output of data shall also be described.

Explanation

This applies to the basic software on the one hand (e.g. operating systems) and the special solution modules on the client side on the other hand.

Normally the documentation of the manufacturer is sufficient to describe the functionality of standard software (data sheets, user manuals, etc.). The versions used shall be recorded and the individual adaptations created by means of customizing shall be described.

If user interfaces have been individually adapted/extended, these shall be mentioned individually.

7.3.10. Special case – individual software

The individual software components that are used shall be described in their entirety. The responsibilities and the processes for change, test and release management are described.

Explanation

This paragraph concerns the functionality of the individual

components that have been developed in-house and go be-yond the standard. The tasks and technical realisation of the respective components must be logical and comprehensible. This applies both to the server and the client-side components of the solution.

Both integration and security aspects are important. Support and error correction measures must be described. In addition, it must be shown how the long-term development is to take place, independently of individual persons.

7.3.11. Interfaces

The interfaces to other integrated and adjacent systems shall be described.

Explanation

Interfaces form a basic quality and security feature within a solution. A detailed and complete description of these is needed. It is recommended that the written description is augmented by a graphic representation which, in particular, clearly shows the connection between the different systems.

7.3.12. Network architecture description

The infrastructure and design of the physical, and if appropriate, virtual network in which the solution is to be operated shall be described.

Explanation

The network components (hardware and software) consti-tute a vital quality characteristic with regard to the security and the performance of a solution. In the case of complex networks, the level of detail of the description is based on the significance of the respective parts of the network for the solution. As a further aid to understanding, the network architecture can also be shown in graphic form if appropriate. Against the backdrop of the security of the documents and their availability, the main emphasis here is also on remote access to the network.

7.3.13. Cloud management

Public, hybrid or multi-cloud infrastructures that are used shall be described.

Explanation

Secure technical linking of the public cloud to the local network of the user organisation (e.g. by means of dedicated cable or VPN) must be described clearly.

It is recommended to create a structure plan for the "virtual network inside the public cloud"; among other things this includes depiction of sub-networks, directory services, security structures and resources used.

In the case that different service models are used in hybrid or multi-cloud operation (IaaS, PaaS or SaaS, etc.) and/or several cloud providers are used, they shall be included in the description.

7.3.14. Electronic signatures, seals and time stamps

The signature, seal and time-stamp technologies that are used and the components associated with them shall be described.

Explanation

Such components include, for example, card readers, signature cards, certificates, software for creation of the signature and signature testing based on existing case law (national and EU).

7.4. Information security

In particular, a suitable Information security concept and plans for data security and data protection are required. Here it is assumed that a general information security concept exists within the organisation which is operating the solution, and that this concept is put into practice (otherwise such a security concept must be established for the introduction of the solution). The audit criteria described here therefore only affect the points which are not already covered by this general security concept.

7.4.1. General information security concept

A general information security concept shall be present and described.

> Explanation
>
> In this concept, all measures are to be described that are used to protect business and personal data appropriately against improper use, change and loss. This includes among others a sufficient risk analysis of the solution as well as the rules and measures that specify how sensitive operating equipment and information are protected.

7.4.2. Specific requirements for the information security concept

The security requirement and the specific risks for the operation of the solution shall be identified. Suitable measures have been taken and are described.

> Explanation
>
> Here, the risks and measures which are relevant to the solution are described in more detail. The security requirement of

the individual components results from the extent to which they are worthy of protection and from a corresponding analysis. The appropriate organisational and technical measures are described on this basis.

In particular, the components relevant to safeguarding, functional capability and orderliness must be taken into consideration (e.g. network, document server, database server and storage systems).

7.4.3. Backup concept

A backup concept is present and is described. Periodic checking of the restore capability is ensured.

Explanation

This concept ensures that all data and documents of the solution can be restored under all circumstances. The concept should be verified by means of tests and modified if necessary.

7.4.4. User administration and authorisation concept

The user administration shall be described, along with the role concept and the access rights. In addition, there is an authorisation concept which is adapted to the legal and internal requirements.

Explanation

Introduction of a solution generally requires specific protective measures as regards data and access protection. In particular, the differences in relation to general IT user administration must be documented.

7.4.5. Entry controls

The measures as regards entry control that are needed for protection of the solution shall be described.

> Explanation
>
> Entry protection is concerned with the physical securing of the data processing equipment in rooms, buildings or other facilities. These include, for example, installation of locking systems which control entry by means of keys, RFID/magnetic cards or biometric features, and also equipment which ensures that individuals can only enter singly (turnstiles, etc.). In general, solutions are operated within the framework of the IT infrastructure and server systems. However, it should be considered if the particular form of the solution in the individual case – e.g. with processing of personal or confidential information – sets special requirements as regards entry control.

7.4.6. Access and data access controls

Special measures for access and data access controls of the solution shall be described.

> Explanation
>
> Access control means authentication of the user when accessing the system with username and identification (e.g. password or two-factor authentication).
> Data access control means controlling the possibilities for entering, reading, changing and deleting the information based on the authorisation concept.
> Remote access and remote maintenance must also be taken into consideration. In particular, those measures that are not

already described in the security concept should be documented.

7.4.7. Transaction, integrity and consistency security

Transaction, integrity and consistency security shall be assured
within the solution and the measures shall be described.

> Explanation
>
> The mechanisms and concepts for transaction, integrity and
> consistency security are described (e.g. in recording scans or
> mass import). The mechanisms ensure that no documents are
> lost, stored twice or changed without authorisation and that
> the correct context of the documents is retained at all times.
> If a component (e.g. OCR) uses the output of an upstream
> component (e.g. scanning solution) as input, completeness
> must be ensured over all documents (e.g. through transfer
> logs, error/defect handling).
> In particular, it must be ensured that any necessary organisa-
> tional measures are described in the documented procedures.

7.4.8. Recording (protocols/logs)

All security-relevant accesses, events, processes or transactions of
the solution shall be logged. The possibility to provide evidence of
the relevant events in the system is guaranteed for the long term.

> Explanation
>
> The depth of logging that is necessary depends on the area
> of use. In some security-sensitive applications, every single
> read and write access or accesses and actions by administra-
> tors must be logged. However, the evaluation of logged data
> must always be considered, particularly with regard to data
> protection and legal requirements (e.g. performance analy-

ses of employees). Parametrisation of the system logging is justified and described.

7.4.9. Safeguarding against failure

The measures for safeguarding against failure shall be described. The measures shall be suitable for ensuring the necessary system availability, even in case of emergency.

Explanation

In particular, it must be shown that the technical and organisational measures taken fulfil the requirements of the intended use of the solution.
Examples of measures intended to achieve security against failure: e.g. cluster systems, cold standby, UPS (Uninterruptible Power Supply), decentralised data backup, etc.
A business continuation plan should be present and contain for example emergency plans, re-start plans and supplier agreements.

7.4.10. Data protection and control measures

Observance of data protection and its implementation and the control measures shall be described.

Explanation

Particular attention must be paid to all data within the solution which allow conclusions to be drawn with regard to natural persons. In addition to data protection law, other rules and regulations must also be taken into consideration, e.g. employee data protection based on industrial relations and labour management law.
The necessary control measures result from the data protection regulations and are generally already covered in the

general information security concept, the data protection concept or in the access protection. For example, the GDPR with the new Federal Data Protection Act (BDSG-neu), which entered into force on 2018-05-25, regulates all measures regarding personal data protection. Therefore only the additional aspects which result from operation of the solution are mentioned here. For example, when external service providers or commissioned data processing are used, it is necessary to conclude suitable contracts for commissioned data processing and/or to implement measures to control orders placed.

Depending on the use case, certified evidence, such as for example according to GDPR (European data protection seal – Art. 42, Certifications) can be useful and appropriate. Orientation regarding possible certifications is provided, for example, by the German Data Protection Conference (DSK).

7.5. Technical operation

The general infrastructure-related and organisational prerequisites for orderly operation of the solution are considered in this section. Technical operation is divided into organisational framework conditions, operating processes within standard operation, and operating processes in emergency scenarios.

Whilst, in standard operation the main focus is on handling of the system and also on monitoring, in the case of defined emergency scenarios fast re-availability of the system and documents must be ensured without loss of data.

In order to ensure the specified availability of the solution, it is necessary to implement preventive servicing and maintenance measures for hardware and software which maintain the status of the system in an appropriate current condition. The maintenance plan describes the time when work is carried out and also the measures performed by internal units and external service providers.

Suitable plans for efficient elimination/correction of disturbances are needed for handling of emergency scenarios.

7.5.1. Responsibilities

The responsibilities in connection with operation of the solution shall be regulated and documented. Work instructions shall exist for employees involved with operating the solution.

> Explanation
> ....
> Documentation of the responsibilities is implemented, for example, by means of organisation charts and role descriptions in the area of IT. The responsibility allocated to each role must be described; in this context, all internal and ex-

ternal persons and organisation units which affect operation of the solution are of interest. Work instructions for standard operation of the solution and for emergency scenarios are present.

7.5.2. Prerequisites with respect to buildings

The necessary prerequisites with regard to buildings shall be present in relation to operation of the solution.

Explanation

The building and office facilities of the user organisation (including any service providers or outsourcers) fulfil the building-related prerequisites for implementation of the other criteria of this section. Items to be considered include, for example, access and entry controls, climate-controlled server rooms, fire protection measures and storage of backup storage media at a separate location.

7.5.3. Operating conditions for hardware

The operating conditions for the hardware shall be fulfilled.

Explanation

The operating conditions result from the manufacturers' information and instructions with regard to the hardware components. This includes for example climate control of server rooms and also regular cleaning of scanners. It is documented that the operating conditions are permanently adhered to.

7.5.4. Operating conditions for software

The operating conditions for the software shall be fulfilled.

The operating conditions (such as for example use of approved operating systems) result from the manufacturers' information regarding the software components. These aspects can be described in the system documentation.

7.5.5. Data backup

An overarching and consistent data backup concept shall be in place. Implementation shall be ensured and monitored.

The data backup concept itself and the description of its content is a component of the information security for all the linked IT systems present in the organisation. At this point, the implementation of the concept in day-to-day operation has to be documented by defined roles or persons.

7.5.6. Handling of storage media

A logical and coherent concept shall be in place for handling and destruction of storage media. Implementation shall be ensured and monitored.

Regardless of what types of storage media are used, rules for the handling of the data carriers in daily operation are made known by means of work instructions or training. Copies created for reasons of security are kept at a separate secure location. Disposal of storage media that are no longer required is also regulated by means of work instructions. Special attention must be paid to data protection here.

7.5.7. Monitoring of orderly operation

Standard operation shall be monitored to ensure orderliness.

Explanation

Arrangements are made for a defined role (represented by a person or group of people) which is responsible for monitoring operation of the system in accordance with the recommendations of the manufacturer or the system integrator. The arrangements include regular checking of the logfiles and journal files and monitoring data, independent of the system or cloud locations, in particular when using cloud scenarios.

7.5.8. Responsibility for maintenance and troubleshooting

The responsibility for maintenance and troubleshooting shall be described and the scope of the work shall be laid down.

Explanation

Depending on the size of the organisation and on the application, this responsibility is carried by IT operation staff, IT development staff or external service providers. The work includes all activities of 1st, 2nd and 3rd tier support, and also management of documents, service agreements, Service-Level Agreements (SLAs), creation and harmonisation of action plans for maintenance and correction of disturbances in collaboration with manufacturers and service organisations, escalation of the maintenance/repair processes if necessary, monitoring the success of maintenance and repair and other arrangements.

7.5.9. Preventive maintenance

Plans for preventive maintenance shall be in place and implemented.

> Explanation
>
> The guidelines of the manufacturers are included in the preventive maintenance plans. One typical preventive maintenance activity is the cleaning of scanner rollers.
> The maintenance plans are agreed with the external service organisations and integrators. Those responsible in the specialist departments are trained in order to perform the maintenance tasks. The success of the maintenance activities is controlled. More extensive and safeguarding maintenance measures performed by external service organisations are described in the maintenance agreement and integrated into the maintenance plan.

7.5.10. Documentation of the maintenance processes

Documentation of the maintenance processes shall be regulated. It shall be ensured that the maintenance processes are documented completely and soon after the processes themselves are carried out.

> Explanation
>
> Documentation of the implementation of the individual maintenance measures includes service reports, protocols/logs, etc.

7.5.11. Troubleshooting

An action plan for reporting and rectifying disturbances shall be in place. The measures are suitable for ensuring the required availability of the system.

Those who are responsible for locating faults are named and an escalation process is defined. Contacts at service providers and also agreed service levels and/or reaction times are laid down. A plan of procedures for restart and recovery is defined.

7.5.12. Restart

Responsibilities and work instructions exist for restart.

By restart is meant the restart of the system following an operational disturbance. A responsible role is defined for the activities of a system restart and a work instruction with corresponding procedures exists.

7.5.13. Recovery

Responsibilities and work instructions shall exist for recovery, in other words the procedure for reinstatement of secured data.

In contrast to restart, in the case of recovery the integrity of the entire system must be reinstated. The procedure must be described in detail.

A responsible role is defined for the activities of a recovery of the system; in addition, work instructions with corresponding procedures and/or an emergency plan are present.

7.5.14. Updating of the hardware

The procedure for updating of the hardware shall be defined and its implementation shall be documented.

7.5.15. Updating of the software

The procedure for updating of the software shall be defined and its implementation shall be documented.

7.6. Long-term availability and migration

Progress (e.g. changes in technology) as well as changes to the legal system and organisation structures can change the factors which determine long-term availability. Therefore there must be a planned, logical, comprehensible and dynamic process which maintains long-term availability on an ongoing basis.

Migration is a part of long-term availability and includes the changes which require transfer of electronic documents and data (e.g. change of system manufacturer, change or replacement of storage formats or the storage solution).

This can involve simple processes such as simple "recopying" of electronic document inventories including the metadata, up to complex processes in which the document formats and metadata structures change.

A suitable procedure for long-term availability includes among other things a migration concept and ensures that both content and also legally required characteristics of the electronic documents and data are retained and manipulation is excluded. In addition, these procedures must be continuously checked to ensure that they are up to date, and they must be modified if necessary.

It is essential that the migration concept, with the associated processes, is described in a migration documentation.

If a migration concept also includes a cloud model, it must be taken into account that data and documents can leave their own legal jurisdiction (e.g. EU) and therefore that legal questions regarding liability can arise.

7.6.1. Concept for long-term availability

There shall be a concept for the long-term availability of documents and the associated data. A description of the capability for long-term availability of the selected data formats, storage media and the hardware and software that are used is an integral part of the concept.

> ## Explanation
> Long-term availability is ensured both through the selection of suitable data formats (e.g. PDF/A) and by the system components (e.g. storage media using standards that are in general use on the market). To these are added the procedures for the storage of metadata, versions, annotations, access rights, history, logs and protocols, etc. Often, the particular concept for long-term availability is augmented or mostly based on documents of the system component manufacturers.

7.6.2. Migration concept

There exists a migration concept for documents and their associated data. A description of the interfaces used for the migration and of the convertibility of the documents and data formats forms an integral part of the concept.

> ## Explanation
> The aspects that are relevant for later migration of the documents and data must be described. Here, both technical and organisational measures must be taken into consideration. The organisational aspects include questions such as the separability of data inventories (e.g. through sale of parts of the organisation, client management, etc.). With regard to the technical aspects, particular attention must be paid to the migration capability of the current solution.

7.6.3. Control

Regular control of the long-term availability and migration capability shall be regulated in a suitable and logical way.

Regular monitoring which is suitable for the task ensures that the long-term availability and the migration capability continue to be guaranteed. This also includes monitoring of technological progress.

The integrity of the documents and data have to be guaranteed over the entire retention period. Each migration involves the risk that the integrity will be destroyed (e.g. through loss of data, manipulation). Documentation of monitoring measures and tests that is validated and suitable for the tasks to be fulfilled ensures trustworthiness and the quality of evidence.

7.6.4. Performing a migration

The performance of a migration shall be documented, including the logs/protocols.

Migration refers to the process of replacing one application with another. The aim is to make all documents and data (e.g. metadata, annotations) available in the new application and to document traceability and completeness of the documents and data at all times.

7.7. Qualification of employees

The operator ensures that all the employees concerned with the system operation have the necessary knowledge and skills. The roles for use of the system and system administration are defined. The corresponding activities and the resulting requirements for the level of knowledge are described for each role. The knowledge of the employees is related to this and documented in a suitable way.

In addition to in-house workers, employees include all external persons who are directly commissioned with processing of data, regardless of whether they are employed at their own operating locations or with service providers or partners working at the operator's site.

7.7.1. Roles
The roles for system use and system administration shall be defined.

Explanation
Typical roles are, for example, users, system administrators, further employees of the IT operation and, if appropriate, external service providers (e.g. for scanning).

7.7.2. Necessary knowledge
The knowledge that is necessary for each role shall be defined.

Explanation
Necessary knowledge generally comprises:
- specialist knowledge of the particular area of application, e.g. knowledge of the relevant accounting areas, for technically correct indexing

- basic IT knowledge and skills which are necessary in order to use the solution, e.g. "general application knowledge" for users from the different areas, or "network administration" for system administrators
- knowledge of the products used, e.g. administration knowledge to the extent offered by a specific training course of the manufacturer
- installation and application-specific knowledge, e.g. knowledge of the different index fields and their significance
- rules and guidelines for orderly system operation, in so far as they affect the special roles

7.7.3. Responsibilities

The operator has named one or several persons to be responsible for employee qualification.

Explanation

These can be different people, depending on the organisation, e.g. the Head of IT can be responsible for qualification of the system administrators, while responsibility for qualification of the system users lies with the individual departments.

7.7.4 Qualification measures

Those responsible within the organisation shall assess, initiate and document the concrete employee qualification measures.

Explanation

The necessary measures result from the requirements of the role on the one hand and the current qualification of the employees (role holders) on the other hand. Possible measures are, for example, instruction by the system integrator, training

by the system integrator or manufacturer, in-house training,
training on the job, webcasts, training videos, etc.
It is important to cover current issues associated with the
role (further qualification).

7.7.5. Documentation of the qualifications and measures

The current qualifications of the individual employees and the
qualification measures shall be appropriately documented.

7.8. Tests

Technically suitable, logical and traceable tests of the solution are of central importance in order to ensure that the core criteria of orderliness, completeness, traceability, immutability, availability and confidentiality are fulfilled. The tests and their documentation cover all systems and processes of the solution to be considered.

7.8.1. Test concept
A complete and consistent test concept shall be provided.

> Explanation
>
> The test concept serves to prove that the technical system and the organisational processes fulfil the core criteria of orderliness, completeness, traceability, immutability and availability. In particular, it describes the different types of tests and/or test levels, test methods used, any test tools used, organisation of tests (rules and regulations, implementation, infrastructures, etc.) and the test materials used.

7.8.2. Test plans and test rules and regulations
Tests shall be planned and designed so as to fulfil the test concept. The desired result shall be defined.

> Explanation
>
> The test plans are drawn from the test concept and control the correct order and concrete use of the test resources. The test specifications and rules cover the entire process, taking all hardware and software components into consideration.

7.8.3. Test protocols

The tests and test results shall be documented by means of test protocols which are signed off by those responsible.

> Explanation
>
> The test protocols document in writing the orderly implementation of the content specified in the relevant test plans, the expected and actual results, and in the case of nonconformities, the actions which are necessary, along with follow-up and control of their implementation.

7.9. Outsourcing

Outsourcing is now common practice when developing and extending solutions. The outsourcing alternatives extend from outsourcing of individual functions (e.g. scanning), individual parts of the process (e.g. preliminary invoice checking), use of software components (e.g. in the form of "Software as a Service") or cloud services (outsourcing of software, infrastructure and platform) up to operation of the entire solution by an external service provider (complete provision of the process steps, including outsourcing of software, infrastructure and platform).

In all cases it must be taken into account that the organisation which uses the solution internally always remains the responsible "operator" of the solution, independently of who in fact provides or operates the individual services or components. Contractual arrangements with third parties do not release the organisation from these obligations.

For this reason, all applicable audit criteria of the AC-DMS must also be applied to the outsourced areas.

7.9.1. Services and responsibility

The services and the responsibilities of the service providers and/ or cloud providers used shall be clearly defined and described.

> Explanation
>
> It must be precisely recognisable how the tasks and responsibilities are divided between the contracting organisation and service providers used and how fulfilment of the core criteria of the AC-DMS is ensured. It may, for example, be possible to see this from the relevant service contracts.
> These must be designed and concluded according to the legal regulations, e.g. by means of assured Service Level Agree-

ments (SLAs). The contracting organisation must in particular specify and define which services the service providers and/ or cloud providers have to supply with regard to the ICS and the process documentation.

7.9.2. Process documentation

Process documentation shall be provided which describes the overall process, including all outsourced components.

Explanation

Orderly process documentation also remains the responsibility of the commissioning organisation in the case of outsourced components. In practice, parts of the documentation are often created and supplied by the service providers and cloud providers involved in the respective process. The commissioning organisation should ensure that the documentation portions contributed by service providers can be understood by third parties and are described in a clear way, and are also updated on a regular basis and in case of changes. It should therefore agree to appropriate rules and documentation guidelines with the service providers and/ or take their rules and guidelines into consideration in its process documentation.

7.9.3. Interfaces

The organisational and technical interfaces shall be listed and described.

Explanation

The complete description of the interfaces is a basic element for the legal certainty and auditability of the solution.
It is a basic prerequisite for smooth and secure communica-

tion between the operator and the service provider.
Organisational interfaces include for example contacts and
contact data of the outsourcing service provider.
In the case of the technical interfaces it must be considered,
if applicable, that there may not only be direct interfaces of
the solution, but also interfaces which are additionally provided by third parties.

7.9.4. Control

Regular assessment of the performance of the outsourcing service
providers shall be defined. The employees and responsibilities on
both sides shall be laid down.

Explanation

It is described how and at what time intervals it is checked
that the service providers provide the specified services as
agreed, and it is confirmed that the evaluation criteria are
always applied.

7.10. Internal Control System (ICS)

The "Internal Control System" (ICS) shall ensure that the core criteria for the solution are adhered to on a continuous basis and that they are regularly checked (orderliness, completeness, traceability, immutability and availability).

The effectiveness of the ICS results from the technical and organisational measures as they are harmonised with one another.

7.10.1. Description of the ICS method

The functioning of the "Internal Control System" with regard to fulfilment of the requirements set for the solution (including legal compliance and auditability) shall be described. The description also covers the interaction of the organisational and technical control measures and their mutual interdependencies.

Explanation

An ICS generally covers the entire structure of an organisation. That part which forms the basis for evidence of the legal certainty and auditability of the solution must be described here. However, the measures of the ICS that are relevant for the solution not only have to take the requirements regarding legal certainty and auditability into consideration, but also all those requirements (legal and internal to the organisation) which result from the area of use and/or the objectives of the solution. For example, in the GDPR, the legislator demands clearly defined responsibilities in order to fulfil the data protection measures. The basis for this is the detailed and structured documentation of the control measures by the responsible persons.

The ICS methods describe and document the interaction between the individual measures in order to guarantee that

fulfilment of the requirements set for the IT system can also
be evidenced to third parties at any time.

7.10.2. Traceability of controls

All controls shall be both progressive and retrospectively traceable.

Explanation

Controls are not an end in themselves, but support orderly
and proper implementation of the rules. Therefore on the
one hand it must be ensured that they are implemented in a
consistent way, and on the other hand they must be transparently traceable. For this reason, it is necessary that controls
can be traced from their beginning to the end (top down)
and also from the end to the beginning (bottom up). This requirement also supports the current nature and consistency
of control sequences.

7.10.3. Documentation of the organisational control measures

The organisational measures and controls for orderly operation of
the solution shall be described.

Explanation

The need for documentation of the organisational control
measures results from the application of the growing compliance requirements. Organisations must ensure adherence
to guidelines – both legal guidelines and those defined by
the organisation – and document these in appropriate detail.
Every larger organisation needs a systematically structured
and sustainably maintained control system. This comprises
on the one hand measures with a preventive function, such

as instruction, information and training provided to employees, but on the other hand assures monitoring and documentation of procedures and events within the organisation itself. A binding set of standards and regulations for documentation of the control measures is essential in this connection.

7.10.4. Documentation of the technical control measures

The technical control measures for orderly operation of the solution shall be described.

Explanation

The way in which protection and security requirements are covered by means of technical measures is shown. This includes, for example, access control, data security and (internal) system logging. It must be ensured that all devices involved in the process, such as mobile end devices, are taken into account.

If hardware, software or infrastructure are provided or implemented by means of a cloud solution, overlapping or overarching legal jurisdictions must be taken into account and suitable agreements must be concluded with the service provider in order to meet the requirements of the home legal jurisdiction and implement the required technical control measures.

7.10.5. Process documentation

The procedure for timely updating of the process documentation and of its storage so as to be secure against manipulation shall be described.

The process documentation must always reflect the current status of the solution.

The solution is generally subject to continual adaptation and modification. The changes associated with this must be recorded chronologically and without gaps, i.e. earlier versions of the process documentation must be retained.

The consistency of the ICS measures must be described on the basis of the current solution.

7.10.6. Control and evaluation of the ICS

The controls of the ICS measures shall be described. The way in which the ICS outputs and results are handled shall be regulated.

The controls of the ICS measures and evaluation of the ICS results and outputs are essential components of the compliance activities throughout the organisation. Needs for action arise from the weaknesses identified by means of the ICS. Implementation of these actions must be guaranteed within day-to-day operation. Ideally, the implementation is structured and follows a rule-based optimisation process (for example PDCA cycle), and the responsibilities are correspondingly regulated and documented.

7.10.7. Assignment of responsibilities

Persons to be responsible shall be assigned to all ICS-relevant measures and actions.

Measures to which no personnel have been assigned in order to take responsibility constitute a weakness. Therefore, this assignment is a vital element for achieving the effectiveness of the ICS and must be assured by means of corresponding measures, e.g. work instructions (see also Process documentation).

Again, orientation on (ISO) standards can be useful, e.g. with implementation of a RACI matrix (responsible-accountable-consulted-informed).

8. Audit and certification

8.1. Introduction

A structure for the solution which conforms with AC-DMS is achieved by means of careful planning, the selection of suitable hardware and software components and by means of suitable operational organisation and creation of process documentation.

Confirmation of conformity can, however, only be performed based on additional assessment by an independent third party and certification by a recognised certification body. In addition, such assessment and certification improve credibility and legal certainty, as the AC-DMS certificate testifies that the technical implementation and the day-to-day processes correspond to the description in the documentation. This also applies in the case of partial certification for any part of the solution under consideration.

VOI (Verband Organisations- und Informationssysteme e.V.) and TÜV Informationstechnik GmbH, TÜV NORD GROUP (TÜVit) have defined a basis for safe and secure use of electronic document management processes and related IT solutions by means of the audit criteria described in this document. The comprehensive experience of VOI and its member companies in the area of conception and implementation of such processes and the long experience of TÜViT in the field of assessment, auditing and certification guarantee the quality of the audit criteria and their technical foundation (AC-DMS).

8.2. Audit and certification options

The following chapters describe the certifications that are possible and also describe the general procedure for the different assessments.

8.2.1. Assessment of a complete solution
Assessment of a "complete solution" is carried out in two stages.

The first stage consists of review of the process documentation. Here, the descriptions contained in the documentation are assessed to establish if they are consistent and complete and fulfil the requirements of the AC-DMS.

The second stage consists of the "practical assessment of the solution" in the form of an on-site audit. An audit team from the certification body verifies the agreement of documentation and technical implementation. In particular, it is assessed if the solution is sufficiently secure against unauthorised access, changes of indexing, falsification of documents and incorrect operation. Spot checks regarding recording, indexing, search and reproduction are carried out for this purpose. Documents are followed on their way through the different stations in the system. The assessment results must be consistent with the facts described in the documentation. In addition, the system environment and conditions under which the solution is used are examined.

8.2.2. Partial certifications
Certification of individual parts of a solution, e.g. document recording/scanning.

In addition to certification of a complete solution it is also possible to certify definable partial solutions, where this is useful and practical. The partial solutions can be provided by independent organisation units or by external service providers.

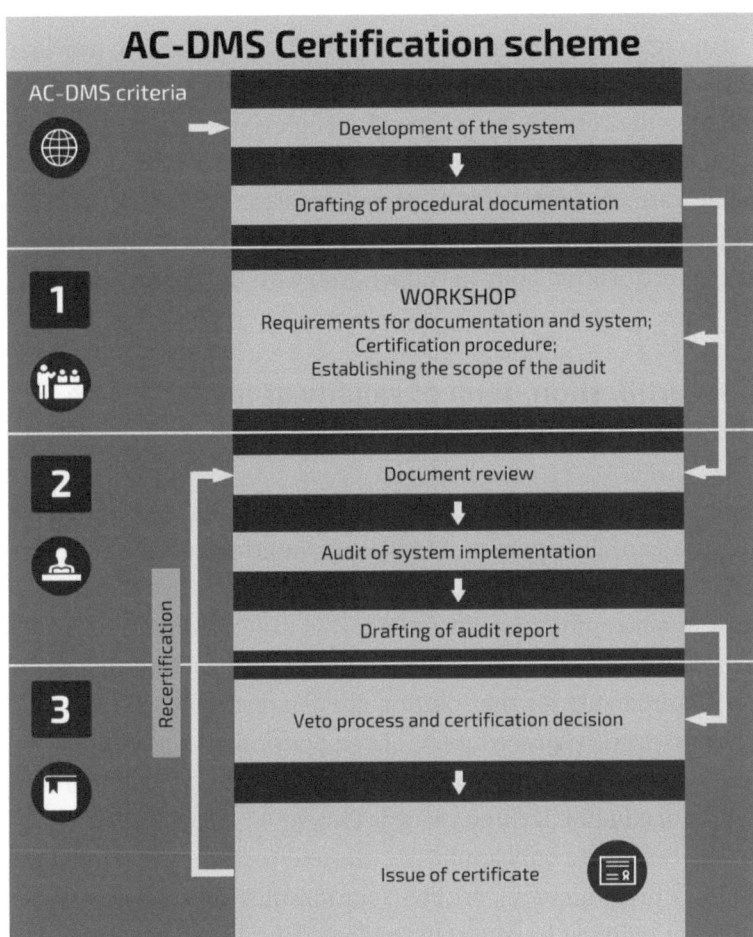

Figure 4 – Schematic diagram of a certification procedure

Independent documentation must be drawn up for the partial solution. The audit and the certification are performed in accordance with the same procedure as for the complete solution. The prerequisites for partial certifications are a clear functional separation as well as defined interfaces. Partial solutions must be declared as such in the documentation.

An organisational unit or an organisation or a service provider who wishes for certification of a partial solution must first precisely define the content and scope of this partial solution. All evaluation areas of the AC-DMS must also be taken into consideration in the case of partial certification. The areas for evaluation and individual criteria for the partial certification shall be determined by the certification body in cooperation with the client.

8.3. Certification, term of validity of the certificate and recertification

The certification decision with issue of the certificate is based on the results of the reviews of the documentation and the practical testing and assessment on site, which are summarised by the auditor in a meaningful audit report. This expert evidence is evaluated by the certification body in a formal certification process. If the requirements for the solution are demonstrably fulfilled, and if the assessment procedure has been performed in a proper manner, a certificate with a defined period of validity, in general two up to a maximum of three years, is issued.

The certificate only applies for the audited solution. Therefore changes to an already-certified solution that are relevant to the certification must be reported to the certification body. The certification body analyses the impacts of the changes and decides on steps, such as for example re-audit, which are necessary in order to maintain the validity of the certificate.

The certification body informs the operator in good time of expiry of the certificate, so that the recertification can follow on seamlessly from the existing certification.

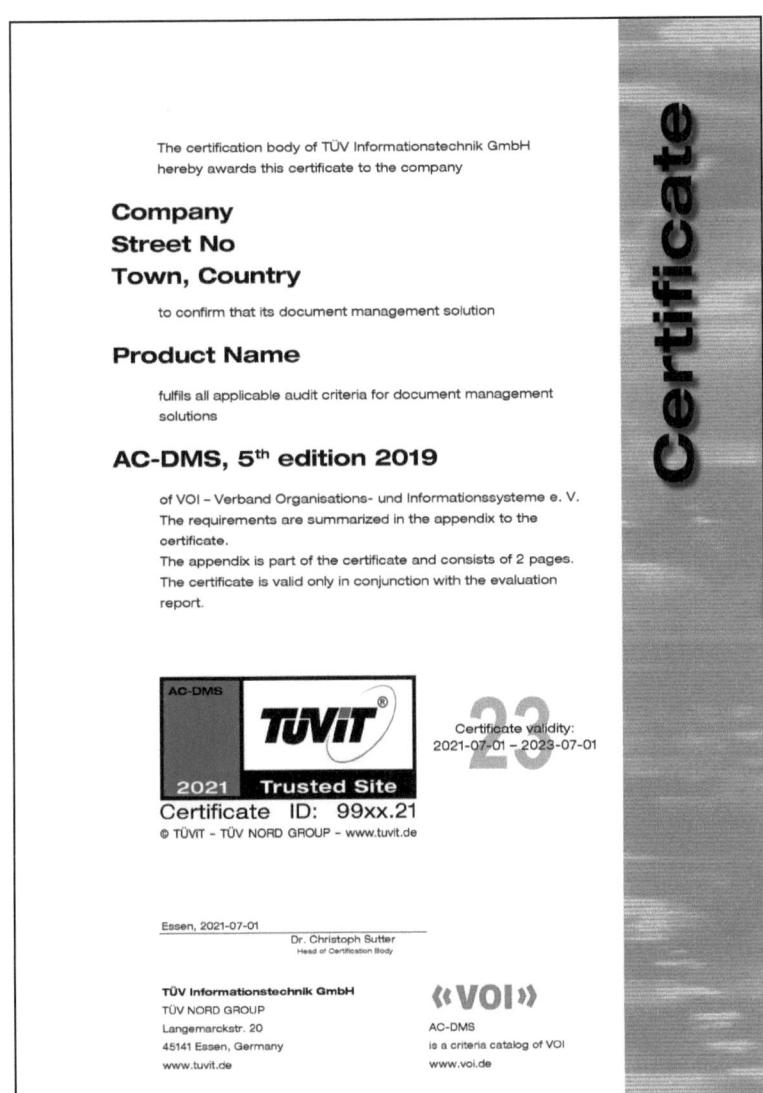

The certification body of TÜV Informationstechnik GmbH hereby awards this certificate to the company

Company
Street No
Town, Country

to confirm that its document management solution

Product Name

fulfils all applicable audit criteria for document management solutions

AC-DMS, 5th edition 2019

of VOI – Verband Organisations- und Informationssysteme e. V. The requirements are summarized in the appendix to the certificate.
The appendix is part of the certificate and consists of 2 pages.
The certificate is valid only in conjunction with the evaluation report.

Certificate validity:
2021-07-01 – 2023-07-01

Certificate ID: 99xx.21
© TÜVIT – TÜV NORD GROUP – www.tuvit.de

Essen, 2021-07-01
Dr. Christoph Sutter
Head of Certification Body

TÜV Informationstechnik GmbH
TÜV NORD GROUP
Langemarckstr. 20
45141 Essen, Germany
www.tuvit.de

《VOI》
AC-DMS
is a criteria catalog of VOI
www.voi.de

Figure 5 - Certificate for an AC-DMS certification of a complete solution

«VOI CERT»

ZERTIFIKAT – CERTIFICATE

Die Zertifizierungsstelle der VOI Service GmbH bescheinigt gemäß VOI-CERT-Regularien dem Softwareprodukt

„System", Revision X

der Firma: Template SE

die Anforderungen nach dem Prüfverfahren „AC-DMS ready" zu erfüllen. Das geprüfte Produkt ermöglicht ein revisionssicheres Compliance-Management digitaler Dokumente.
Der Nachweis wurde durch das Prüfverfahren mit der Nummer VCC21000 erbracht.

Das Gütezeichen VOI Compliance Certificate (VCC) „Geprüfte Sicherheit" wurde erteilt.

VOI Service GmbH Certification Authority certifies according to the VOI-CERT Certification and Testing Regulation that the software product

"System", Revision X

from: Template SE

fulfills the requirements of the "AC-DMS ready" specification. The tested product permits an auditable Compliance Management of digital documents. A Certification Process was performed with Report No. VCC21000 and proof has been provided that the requirements are fulfilled.

The approval mark VOI Compliance Certificate (VCC) "Tested Security" has been granted.

VOI Compliance Certificate
„AC-DMS ready"

Datum der Zertifizierung:	01.03.2021	Date of Certification:	2021-03-01
Prüfberichtnummer:	VCC21000	Audit Report No.:	VCC21000
Zertifikatnummer:	ZVCC21000	Certificate No.:	ZVCC21000
Zertifikat gültig für:	Revision X	Certificate valid for:	Revision X

VOI Service GmbH - Zertifizierungsstelle
Bonn, den 01.03.2021

VOI Service GmbH
Certification
Authority
Bonn 2021-03-01

Peter J. Schmerler
Geschäftsführer / Managing Director

VOI Service GmbH—Zertifizierungsstelle, Postfach 140 231, D-53057 Bonn, T. 0228 908 2089, F. 0228 908 2091, voi@voi.de, www.voi.de

Figure 6 – Certificate for AC-DMS certification of a partial system or solution

8.4. Responsibilities

8.4.1. Steering committee
The steering committee is the body that makes decisions regarding the development, maintenance and updating of the AC-DMS and the associated auditing and certification procedure.

The tasks of the steering committee include:

- approval of the current list of criteria and later versions
- approval of procedures for auditing and certification

The members of the steering committee are as follows:

- VOI e.V. – represented by the top management and also the chairperson of the VOI AC-DMS steering committee and his deputy
- TÜV Informationstechnik GmbH (employees of the certification body)

Cooperation partners may also participate in so far as this seems helpful for the further development and wide-ranging acceptance of the AC-DMS (e.g. discussion and agreement with other auditing bodies and industry associations).

8.4.2. Working group
The working group has the following tasks.

- ongoing development of the audit and certification criteria
- preparation of bases of decisionmaking for the steering committee (content, procedures, descriptions, etc.)

The working group is organised by VOI and composed of its various members. Up to two employees from TÜViT can participate.

8.4.3. Certification body

The certification body approves the auditors and lays down the approval conditions. The certification body assigns the audit teams to the individual certifications to be conducted.

The certification body makes the certification decision based on the audit report which was drawn up by the audit team. In the case of a positive decision, the certification body issues the certificate and, upon request of the operator, publishes it on its website. The certification body informs the operator in good time of expiry of the certificate, so that a recertification audit can be performed promptly.

For certification of both complete and partial solutions, the certification body is obliged to carry out the certification in accordance with DIN EN ISO/IEC 17065; at the same time, the certification body is obliged to maintain confidentiality in relation to third parties.

9. General

9.1. Scope of the criteria

The criteria described in this document apply for complete solutions and partial solutions in connection with digital document management processes and associated IT solutions of all kinds.

9.2. Responsibilities and addresses

9.2.1. Certification Body of TÜViT

TÜV Informationstechnik GmbH –TÜV NORD GROUP
Langemarckstraße 20
D-45141 Essen, Germany
www.tuvit.de

Contact:

Tobias Kippert
E-Mail: T.Kippert@tuvit.de
Tel.: +49 201 8999 546
Fax: +49 201 8999 666

9.2.2. Certification Body of VOI (VOI-CERT)

VOI Verband Organisations- und Informationssysteme e. V. –
voice of information
Certification Body VOI-CERT VOI Service GmbH
Heilsbachstr. 25
D-53123 Bonn, Germany
www.voi-cert.de

Contact:

Peter J. Schmerler
(Managing Director of VOI e.V. and VOI Service GmbH)
E-Mail: peter.schmerler@voi.de
Tel.: +49 228 908 2089
Fax: +49 228 908 2091

Dr. Klaus-Peter Elpel
E-Mail: k-p.elpel@voi.de
Mobile: +49 160 96382585

Ralf Kaspras
E-Mail: r.kaspras@voi.de
Mobile: +49 172 4512733

9.2.3. Working Group

VOI Verband Organisations- und Informationssysteme e. V. –
voice of information
VOI e.V.
Heilsbachstr. 25
D-53123 Bonn. Germany
www.voi.de

Contact:

Ralf Kaspras
E-Mail: r.kaspras@voi.de
Mobil: +49 172 4512733

9.3. Waiver

VOI e.V. does not accept liability or offer a guarantee for the correctness and/or completeness of the contents of this document. VOI e.V. cannot accept any legal responsibility or liability whatsoever for incorrect or incomplete information or its consequences. Furthermore, VOI e.V. retains the right to revise the criteria in the document for technical reasons and to make changes.

10. Glossary

Acceptance
See →*Audit*

Accreditation
By accreditation is meant the formal listing and authorisation of an auditor by the certification body. With the accreditation, the certification body acknowledges both the technical competence and the independence of the auditor.

Action
Synonym: Process step
An action is a closed group of activities, which, with a certain input and a certain output, is part of a process. Actions are also designated as process steps and are the lowest non-divided level in the process diagrams.

Annotation
Synonym: Comment, note, remark
Remarks, mostly in text or graphic form, which are digitally generated in connection with the processing of a document and are administered in the →*DMS* together with the document. The content of the document itself is not changed.

AO
Federal Fiscal Code (German: Abgabenordnung)

Archiving

This refers to a form of storage that protects the objects to be stored from alteration or untraceable removal.

Attribute

Synonym: Key, keyword, index
Identifying or descriptive characteristic of a document, so that it can be found again (→*Retrieval*).

Attribute allocation

Synonym: Provide with key words, index, qualify
Provide a document with attribute values.

Audit

In the present list of the criteria, the word audit is taken to mean the inspection of a document management solution of an operator. The audit of a solution comprises:

1. Review of the process documentation for formal completeness and adherence to the criteria.

2. System audit at the operator's premises, in which the agreement of the real system with the process documentation is assessed.

An audit is a determination of the actual state of a concrete IT document management system (object of audit) performed by an independent audit team. Based on a criteria list, a set and actual comparison is carried out and the result is recorded in an →*Audit* Report.

Audit Management

The audit management is located at the approved certification bodies and is responsible for the organisation of the entire audit and certification process. It plans the audits, informs the operators with regard to the inspection and certification procedure and makes the necessary arrangements with the operator.

Audit report

An audit report summarises the assessment results and formulates the recommendation of the audit team for the certification body.

Audit Team

An audit team conducts audits and writes audit reports. It is composed of one or several persons who have proven their qualification for the task to the certification body and who have to be authorised by the body.

Auditor

An auditor assesses a solution of an operator based on defined audit criteria. The auditor is approved by the certification body following demonstration of his qualification and is a part of the audit team.

Barcode

Very reliable machine-readable script, scanned using an opto-electronic process. The set of characters is coded by means of bars and spaces of different widths (1D barcode) or in the form of matrices with a light-dark raster (2D barcode). There are various types of coding; some of these can be used universally, whilst others are reserved for special applications. As information in 1D barcodes is coded in the width of the bars and the spaces, minimum requirements as regards resolution must be adhered to both in the printing and in the reading/scanning of barcodes. Barcodes are often used in the DMS environment in order to identify paper slips of various types clearly and to assign them automatically following scanning.

Certification

Certification is a process performed by a neutral third party which demonstrates reasonable confidence that a product or system that is designated in specific fashion is in agreement with a corresponding rule or regulation. Such rules and regulations are, for example, directives, standards and generally recognised guidelines. In the case of AC-DMS certification, the auditability of the document management solution (system designated in a specific fashion is confirmed in accordance with the AC-DMS criteria (as a recognised standard).

Follow-up certification

Additions and changes to the document management solutions which are relevant to auditability can be inspected and assessed in a follow-up certification process in order to adapt the scope of the certificate to the current solution.

Re-certification

Renewed auditing of the document management solution (structure and operation) following expiry of the certificate.

CI

Coded Information
Information which is coded and which is generally easy to process further by means of machine. This term does not specify the type of coding. One of the most widely used codes for text in the world of IT is the ASCII format. The concept "CI" is generally used in order to differentiate from →*NCI*, in other words non-coded information (e.g. raster images).

Cloud Computing

A form of outsourcing of IT services, data and documents

COLD

Computer Output on Laser Disc
Direct storage of computer-generated data such as outgoing mail, print lists, etc. in a digital archive. COLD data were often archived on optical discs in the past, which explains the name.

Company-specific Security Policy

A collection of guidelines and rules which specify how assets (financial and material assets and sensitive information) are handled and protected within the operating organisation.

Compliance

Adherence to laws, directives, guidelines and other rules of behaviour which must be applied by an organisation. A →*DMS* which is operated or assessed according to the AC-DMS constitutes an important component within the framework of corporate compliance, as all relevant documents are stored in a way which is auditable, and access to them is assured.

Compound Document

Document consisting of several individual objects and whose cohesion and integrity is ensured by functions of a DMS

Confidentiality

An object is confidential if it should not be viewed by anyone and everyone. Within a DMS, confidential objects are protected by the user administration and corresponding access authorities.

Criteria

By criteria is meant here the minimum requirements for a solution.

Customizing

Customer-specific configuration and adaptation of a system, however without changing the program code

DMS

Document management solution
See →*DMS = Document Management System* (below)

DMS

Document management system
By DMS in the widest sense is meant an IT system for the recording, storage, archiving, processing, onward transfer, search and reproduction of documents, see also →*ECM*

Document

Synonym: Electronic document
A document is a compilation of information for a particular purpose on any type of data carrier. It is closed from the point of view of content in the sense of purpose-related indivisibility. A document can contain all kinds of digital information and can consist of one or several individual objects (e.g. images, datasets, texts or tables). See also Chapter 4.2.1 Document

DP

Data processing
Somewhat obsolete traditional term. Has been mostly replaced by the concept →*IT/Information Technology.*

ECM

Enterprise Content Management
Generic term for the technologies used for recording, administration, storage, archiving and provision of content and documents in order to support organisational processes, see also →*DMS* = *Document Management System* (above).

eIDAS

"electronic IDentification, Authentication and trust Services" – Regulation (EU) No 910/2014 of the European Parliament and of the Council of 23 July 2014 on electronic identification and trust services for electronic transactions in the internal market and repealing Directive 1999/93/EC. This regulation led to replacement of →*SigG* and →*SigV*. Among others, electronic seals were introduced →*Electronic Seal*.

EIM

Enterprise Information Management
EIM is a further development of →*ECM* and supports the approach for integrated and structured management and organisation of structured and unstructured information in a company or other institution, etc. Components of EIM are among others also communication, cooperation and process orientation.

Electronic Seal

Standardised technical procedure which proves the authenticity and integrity of signed data. Electronic seals are based on certificates for legal persons. The rules governing this are laid down in EU Regulation 910/2014 (→*eIDAS*) and correspond to those for an →*Electronic Signature*.

Electronic Signature

Standardised technical signature procedure which proves the authenticity and integrity of the signed data. Electronic signatures are based on certificates for natural persons and can be of equal status to hand-written signatures within European jurisdiction. The processes which are necessary for this are laid down in EU Regulation 910/2014 (→*eIDAS*). In association with →*VDG*, this regulation replaces the Federal Signature Act →*SigG*. In some areas of the law, e.g. the eGovernment Act (eGovG) electronic signatures are already a legal requirement.

Evaluation Criteria

See →*Minimum Requirements*

GoBD

Basic principles for orderly management and storage of accounts books, records and documents in electronic form and also data access (Letter of the German Finance Ministry (BMF) of 14.11.2014) Replaces the basic principles of orderly DP-supported accounting systems (GoBS of 1995) and also the "Basic principles of data access and auditability of digital records" (BMF letter of 17 July 2001).

HGB

Federal Commercial Code – (German: Handelsgesetzbuch)
Rules for the storage of documents can be found mainly in the third book (trading books), in the first section (Rules for all traders – German: Vorschriften für alle Kaufleute) in Art. 239, Clause 2 HGB and Art. 239 HGB.

ICR

Intelligent Character Recognition
Generic term for methods for recognising or classifying texts in addition to pure character recognition (→OCR). In the case of ICR, further reference information, and if necessary field and form definitions or external databases are consulted in order to increase the interpretation capability and success rate. It is also used to classify document contents more effectively in comparison to pure OCR by using rules or statistical procedures.

ICS

Internal Control System (general)
The totality of all harmonised controls, measures and rules used for adherence to relevant requirements within operational processes. The ICS logic can be understood from a logical point of view and is also consistent.

IS

Information Security

IT

Information Technology

IP

Information Processing

Jukebox

Robotic system for replaceable media such as optical discs, tapes, etc.

List of Criteria

The present list and description of criteria of the AC-DMS forms the basis for auditing and certification.

Mailbox

Synonym: Work list, task list
Digital folder in which documents to be processed are located. Mailboxes can be assigned to individual persons (individual mailbox) or groups (group mailboxes).

Migration

Updating of data recording; because of the ongoing changes in technology or limited lifetime of the storage media, it is essential to migrate archived data, for example, from time to time, in other words to transfer it to other systems. For the user this means that data should be prepared in such a way that they can be transferred from an existing data carrier to any others without difficulty and without loss of data. In contrast to this "data carrier migration", in the considerably more complex "system migration" all data and existing documents are migrated to another DMS product. Change of hardware and operating system platforms is also designated "migration".

Minimum Requirements

Minimum requirements are understood to be the minimum requirements as regards the orderliness of a solution. The minimum requirements are so-called "KO" criteria, i.e. all minimum requirements must be fulfilled in order that a certificate can be issued.

Monitoring

Monitoring is a particular type of recording within a DMS/ERP system. The monitoring function consists in intervening in a procedure or process which is under observation in a regulating sense, if the procedure or process is not taking the required course or if certain limit values are not reached or are exceeded.

NAS

Network-Attached Storage
Storage technology based on hard drives which facilitates direct access to data stored in a local network without a dedicated server, and which therefore helps to reduce installation and administration costs. NAS is being used more and more frequently as an alternative to →*Jukeboxes* for mass storage and archiving (see also →*SAN*).

NCI

Non-Coded Information
Non-coded information which cannot be further processed directly by the computer (e.g. images, tone sequences, raster graphics, e.g. scanned documents or videos). Content of NCI documents or information carriers can only be further processed by a computer following suitable conversion (e.g. →*OCR*).

OCR

Optical Character Recognition
Initially name for process for recognising standardised OCR A (only upper case letters) and OCR B-font (both upper and lower case letters) using optical reading units. Today this concept is used to describe recognition of machine or hand-written characters from a (preferably) black and white raster image through analysis of light and dark areas. The signs that are recognised are converted into machine-readable text characters and are therefore available for further machine processing.

Onward transfer

Sending on of documents into the digital mailbox of a member of staff or an organisation unit for further processing of the particular matter in hand

Operational Procedure

By operational procedure is meant the entire organisational sequence of business processes or events, which can contain one or several workflows.

Operator

The operator is taken to mean the organisation which operates a solution and initiates the audit and certification procedure by sending an enquiry to the audit management. If the application is outsourced to third parties (e.g. a data centre), the identity of the operator in the legal sense does not change.

PDF

Portable Document Format
Data format from the company Adobe, which is based on the printer control language "Postscript", and which enables generation, administration and viewing of documents independently of any particular platform. PDF files enable presentation of content which is demanding from the graphics point of view and at the same time enable functions like text search, text selection or the integration of interactive elements. PDF Version 1.7 is internationally standardised as ISO 32000-1:2008.

PDF/A

Standard first published in ISO 19005-1:2005 for long-term archiving of electronic documents. PDF/A-1 is based on PDF Version 1.4. In June 2011, PDF 2-A followed in ISO 19005-2:2011. The specification of PDF 3-A has been available since October 2012.

Process

Repeated activity consisting of several individual steps and performed by persons and/or IT systems. Examples of processes are the scanning and transfer on of documents.

Process Documentation

The documentation of the entire solution created by the operator with all relevant technical and organisational aspects. Among other things, it completely describes all the operating processes from recording through storage up to reproduction of the documents.

Process documentation forms the basis for a certification process. Process documentation is stated by the GoBS (principles of orderly EDP-supported bookkeeping systems) to be essential for storage of documents which are tax-relevant and relevant to matters of trade in a DMS.

Proof Capability

An IT system possesses proof capability if it can be proven that the documents within it are recorded, stored, processed, archived and deleted in a correct and orderly fashion. This results on the one hand from system characteristics and organisational processes which can be tracked without doubt and which are protected against undesired changes and manipulations in a defined fashion. On the other hand, recording of the concrete processes within an IT system makes a decisive contribution to proof capability.

Rendition

Synonym: Incarnation

Documents with identical content, but in a different format or medium. A document can, for example, be available in several renditions in different formats (TIFF, PDF, MS-Word file and paper printout).

Reporting

DMS/ERP function, which creates automatically generated reports with content defined in advance

Retrieval

Synonym: Search

Search for and access to →*Documents*, document groups or parts of documents

Role

A role is represented by at least one natural person, who is then the owner of the role. All owners of a role have the same task or relationship to the system. Examples of roles are system administrator and scan operator.

SAN

Storage Area Network

Network between servers and (any type of) storage media, in which access to memory content is performed with an optimised protocol: block-based access in contrast to file-based access in an LAN (Local Area Network). An SAN permits the development of fail-safe storage over different locations and can therefore also be designed so as to be disaster-tolerant. An →*NAS* can access (widely spread) memory resources via an SAN.

SigG

Federal Signature Act

The Federal Act referring to framework conditions for electronic signatures (German: Signaturgesetz - SigG) regulates technical and organisational framework conditions for the use of electronic processes to render a signature (→*Electronic Signature*). Replaced by the →*elDAS* Regulation and the →*VDG*.

SigV

German Signature Ordinance which applies the Signature Act in concrete form and augments it. Replaced by →*elDAS* Regulation and the →*VDG*.

System development

This concept is used in the IT world for the process of program development, maintenance and installation and covers the process and personnel-related aspects.

Test

Tests define the processes used for testing a solution. They must be documented in full and describe the correct mode of functioning. Tests are only useful if the test criteria have been fully defined in advance.

Trustworthiness

Characteristic of solutions which expresses the level of trust that can be placed in the security provided by the object of the audit.

TÜViT

TÜV Informationstechnik GmbH – TÜV NORD GROUP

TÜViT is a member of the TÜV NORD GROUP and has its headquarters in Essen, Germany. The certification body of TÜViT certifies solutions in accordance with the AC-DMS criteria and publishes the certificates on its website. Furthermore, TÜViT supplies members of staff as auditors for the audit process.

UPS

Uninterruptible power supply
An emergency power supply by means of which an IT system is either shut down in a controlled way or can continue to be operated using an independent power supply until the public mains power supply is restored. Such an arrangement in the first instance avoids loss of data and enables rapid re-start. The second solution suggested above offers greater availability of the IT system.

VDG

Federal Trust Services Act (Vertrauensdienstegesetz – VDG)
Forming part of the eIDAS implementation act, VDG implements the national aspects of the →*eIDAS* regulation, such as for example the responsible regulatory body.

Viewer

A special image viewing program by means of which documents stored in a DMS can be displayed with their →*Annotations*, stamps and versions; also generally provided with an automatic page preview ("Thumbnails").

VOI

VOI – voice of information – Verband Organisations- und Informationssysteme e. V., Bonn: www.voi.de. VOI is the specific sector association for suppliers and users of all kinds of electronic document processes. These include among others the areas of electronic document management and archiving (DMS), Enterprise Content Management (ECM) and Enterprise Information Management (EIM).The main areas of activity of VOI include the development of "Best Practice" recommendations and standards and design of legal certainty and auditability.

VOI CERT

Certification body of VOI e.V., Bonn, Germany

Workflow

Synonym: Business incident, event, work sequence
A Workflow is a process built up of individual activities which are related to parts of a business process or other organisational events.

Workflow management system

Synonym: WfMS
A program system (software) for the definition and control of workflows

Working group

VOI and TÜViT develop and update the audit criteria described in this document in an ongoing process in the AC-DMS working group.

WORM

Write Once Read Many
Storage media and storage systems which secure the immutability and proof against deletion of previously stored information in a closed system by means of the physical attributes of the medium or by means of secure software are designated as WORM (Write Once Read Many).

WpHG

Federal Securities Trade Act
(German: Wertpapierhandelsgesetz)

11. Annex

11.1. Other quality assurance standards with points of contact to the AC-DMS

The AC-DMS makes it possible to increase auditability and legal certainty within the framework of business activities. It has points of contact with other quality management systems. Some of the most important of these are described below.

If an organisation makes use of several such systems, the importance of harmonised interaction of those responsible for them increases. The most vital aspects are those of avoiding redundancies and minimising the costs and time involved.

IT-Grundschutz (BSI)

By means of IT Basic Security (German: IT Grundschutz), the Federal Office for Information Security (BSI) aims – based on the definition of an item to be investigated (e.g. a technical task, a business process or an organisation unit) – to define its IT network or "domain" as the sum of information technology (IT) components related to the item, to then establish a protection requirement, and to develop a standard security level for IT systems by means of infrastructure-related, organisational, personnel and IT-related standard security measures. It provides a technically driven approach in which the IT service assets are centre stage. In autumn 2017 the results of a basic modernisation of the IT Grundschutz methods were presented, which since 01 February 2018 have been available as a Compendium within the BSI 200.2 Standard and as from September 2018 these have been the only binding audit basis for certifications to ISO/IEC 27001 on the basis of IT-Grundschutz.

With the introduction of the new 200 standard, IT Grundschutz was completely revised and, among other changes, restructured with differentiation between separate modules for process and system. The contents were given greater focus and new themes such as IoT appliances and equipment (IoT: Internet of Things) and „Industrial IT" were included. The differentiation between basic, core and standard security, which in particular takes the needs of SMEs into account and makes it possible for them to secure their most important assets ("crown jewels"), despite generally only having a limited budget available for questions of information security.

The process was streamlined and can now be implemented more flexibly. The new process steps are as follows: IT structure analysis, defining protection needs, modelling, IT Grundschutz check (replaces basic security check), risk analysis and additional security safeguards (replaces additional security analysis) as well as implementation of IT security measures.

The IT Grundschutz methodology augments the procedure according to ISO/IEC 27001 and provides a good basis on the operative technical level, which in turn ensures a high level of effectiveness for implementation of the measures. Certification according to IT Grundschutz alone is no longer possible; it can only be granted by the Federal Office for Information Security (BSI) in association with ISO/IEC 27001, on the basis of IT Grundschutz. Assessments which are performed solely according to IT Grundschutz are recognised in the form of two auditor attestations, the "IT-Grundschutz Entry Level" and "IT-Grundschutz Secondary Level" (for which the BSI 200 standard also applies as a binding basis as of September 2018).

ISO/IEC 27001

The objective of ISO/IEC 27001 is to create comprehensive information security management systems within organisations/companies which ensure that information security (mainly in the form of availability, integrity and confidentiality of assets) is adequately considered in all internal structures and processes of the organisation. ISO/IEC 27001 defines internationally valid and comparable requirements for this purpose (in the form of control objectives, also referred to as "controls"), according to which certification of the organisation is possible. Starting from a risk assessment which considers the primary information assets (business processes and associated data) and the service-orientated information assets (such as for example hardware, software, network, personnel, location and organisation), handling measures are planned, implemented, monitored and improved. ISO 17799 (renamed ISO/IEC 27002 in 2007), which is compatible with the structure of ISO 27001, serves the organisation as an operative addition in the sense of a best practice approach.

ISO/IEC 27002

ISO/IEC 27002 augments all controls listed in the normative Annex A "List of controls and their objectives" of ISO/IEC 27001 with further specifications and a suite of proposals for the implementation of all requirements for information security management systems in the sense of ISO/IEC 27001. The supportive nature of ISO/IEC 27002 is illustrated by the fact that requirements are mostly formulated as recommendations rather than binding rules and can be supplemented by bespoke controls, which shows that this standard has been designed as an addition to or further specification of ISO/IEC 27001.

ISO/IEC 27017 and ISO/IEC 27018

As shown by the official title of ISO/IEC 27017 ("Code of practice for information security controls based on ISO/IEC 27002 for cloud services"), this ISO standard is based on the same framework as ISO/IEC 27002, adapting and augmenting it by seven new controls which cover cloud-sector specific information security requirements.

ISO/IEC 27018 ("Code of practice for protection of personally identifiable information (PII) in public clouds acting as PII processors"), on the other hand, is mainly a reaction to the requirements (formulated, among others, by the GDPR) with regard to the protection of personally identifiable information in (public) cloud services. Just like ISO/IEC 27017 it introduces a number of completely new controls which must be taken into account in the certification of cloud systems.

However neither ISO/IEC 27017 nor 27018 are complete management standards like ISO/IEC 27001. Therefore they should be seen as additions to ISO/IEC 27001 certifications.

CobiT
(Control Objectives for Information and Related Technology)

The intensive use of IT for support and implementation of processes which are relevant to business means that it is necessary to establish a suitable control environment. CobiT has been developed by ISACA (Information Systems Audit and Control Association, http://www.isaca.org) as a method of assessing the completeness and effectiveness of such a control environment in order to limit any risks that may occur. CobiT identifies the following target groups:

- management – to offer support in decisions involving the balance between risks and the investment needed for control measures
- users – to enable better evaluation of the reliability and control of IT services which are provided internally or by third parties
- auditors – for factual underpinning of audit statements or in the course of consultancy with regard to development and operation of internal controls and
- staff responsible for processes or IT – to offer support during their work

When using CobiT, the user first establishes the IT processes that are relevant for the concrete situation. For each control objective of the selected IT processes, a decision then has to be made as to how far the existing measures fulfil the requirements. CobiT differentiates between seven different business requirements and groups these into the three categories of quality, security and orderliness.

ITIL (IT Infrastructure Library)

ITIL is a widely used basis for the implementation of IT Service Management (ITSM). The processes necessary for operation of an IT infrastructure, the structural organisation and the tools are described. Continual service improvement, operative service operation, commissioning, framework conditions for service development and service strategy are discussed in several books.

The ITIL is based on the added business value to be supplied to the client by IT operation. Planning, provision, support and efficiency optimisation of IT service performance with regard to their use as relevant factors in order to achieve the business goals of a company are considered.

Requirements for bookkeeping by means of IT

Record-keeping for IT compliance started with DP-supported bookkeeping, which continues to occupy a key position among the possible applications. The starting point is comprehensive process documentation which pays particular attention to the specific legal requirements for bookkeeping and tax reporting.

In Germany, for example, the GoBD (requirements regarding orderly DP-supported bookkeeping systems, decree by the Federal Ministry of Finance of 14.11.2014) currently govern basic formal requirements such as minimum standards for the contents of a set of process documentation.

In addition to these documents, rules specific to an industry association can also play an important role. In Germany, the Institut der Deutschen Wirtschaftsprüfer IDW (German: Institute of Public Auditors) has issued various statements regarding invoicing which embody similar principles. In the publications "IDW RS FAIT 1-3", principles of orderly bookkeeping with the use of information technology, electronic commerce and electronic archiving processes are formulated.

ISO 9000

The purpose of the ISO 9000 family of standards is to define requirements regarding a quality management system. Fulfilment of these requirements has to be documented by an organisation in order to demonstrate its ability to fulfil customer requirements and to enable assessment of this ability by internal and external bodies. In addition, it is assessed whether the IT landscape in the organisation fulfils customer requirements and is suitable for the particular business purpose. The purpose of this standard is not to indicate the uniform nature of quality management systems. The concept and the implementation of a quality management system for an organisation are influenced by the organisation's objectives, the particular customer requirements and the products, services or processes on offer.

ISO 19600 Compliance management systems

Rather than stipulating requirements, ISO 19600 contains recommendations as well as proven and tested practices for the design of compliance management systems. It has been created with the possibility of combining it with other management standards, such as for example ISO 9000, in mind. In principle it follows the idea of continual improvement according to the plan-do-check-act method.

TR-RESISCAN

The Technical Regulation (German: Technische Richtlinie) BSI TR-03138 (RESISCAN) in Version 1.4.1 (23.04.2020) describes requirements for reliable technical realisation of replacement scanning, so that the original can then be destroyed. Therefore certification to this standard is a process certification. The regulation consists of a main document, an obligatory audit specification in Version 1.3 and further informative documents.

Very strict methodology is used in the implementation of the TR. A structural analysis is followed by the protection requirement analysis. After this, the resulting security measures are developed, which are then consolidated in a modular list of requirements.

This means that the scanning process is structured based on the protection requirements for the documents to be scanned which resulted from the protection requirement analysis (normal, high, very high). Basic technical and organisational measures are defined (normal). For high and very high protection requirements, further secondary measures for availability, integrity and confidentiality are defined.

The downstream DMS and the archive are not the object of the TR. However, the TR does contain requirements regarding the scan software and scanner used in the process, but without going as far as prescribing the use of a specific type of replacement scanner. This TR in particular does not regulate the permissibility of the scanning which is to replace paper versions as such. This has to be considered individually depending on the area of use, based on the current legal rules and regulations. Nevertheless, reference is made to the applicability of TR RESISCAN in the German eGovernment Act (eGovG), among others.

TR-ESOR

With the Technical Regulation (German: Technische Richtlinie) BSI-TR 03125 "Preservation of Evidence of Cryptographically Signed Documents" (TR-ESOR) in Version 1.2.1 (15.03.2018), the Federal Office for Information Security provides guidance which describes how electronically signed data and documents can be stored in a trustworthy fashion that preserves their value as evidence over long periods of time until the end of their retention period.

There are three levels of conformity that apply to TR-ESOR products.

- Level 1: Functional conformity (only external interfaces are tested)
- Level 2: Technical conformity (modules and interfaces are tested)
- Level 3: Conformity with the German Federal Agency Profiling (staged requirements)

EU Regulation 910/2014 (eIDAS) and Federal Trust Services Act (VDG)

EU Regulation 910/2014 (eIDAS) has been in force since 1 July 2016 and applies all over the European Union. In addition, the Federal Trust Services Act (VDG) – implemented as part of the eIDAS Implementation Act – governs the national aspects of the eIDAS Regulation. For example, it stipulates that the supervisory authority is the Federal Network Agency, except in the case of website certificates, where the Federal Office for Information Security is the supervisory authority. The regulation also renders the Federal Signature Act (SigG) and the Signature Ordinance (SigV) invalid.

The eIDAS Regulation governs electronic identities and trust services. Rules and regulations regarding electronic identities belong to the sphere of public authority and are intended to ensure and legally regulate the interoperability of the different, national identification systems (the new identity card or the electronic residence permit in Germany, for example).

The following services are defined in the field of trust services:

- electronic signatures (for natural persons)
- electronic seals (for legal persons)
- electronic time stamps (proof of time)
- website certificates (authentication of website operators)
- validation service for signatures (verification of signatures and seals)
- delivery of electronic registered mail (De-Mail in Germany, for example)
- Preservation service (preservation of the proof capability of signatures, seals and time stamps and thus an alternative to TR-ESOR).

These services are offered and provided both by non-qualified and qualified trust service providers. The requirements for these trust service providers are also defined in the Regulation. All qualified trust services and trust service providers are published in an EU trust list.

DIN 31644

DIN 31644 is a framework standard and formulates 34 criteria for trustworthy digital long-term archives in libraries and also for commercial enterprises. The criteria are divided into three parts: Organisation, Management of digital objects and their representation, and Infrastructure and Security.

GDPR/BDSG-neu

The General Data Protection Regulation is part of the EU data protection reform presented by the European Commission on 25 January 2012. The General Data Protection Regulation is directly applicable in all EU member states as of 25 May 2018.

The GDPR does not fundamentally change the concept nor, to a large extent, the detailed regulations of current data protection law. Instead, many of the provisions of the EC Data Protection Directive 95/46 are taken over, so that these also form the basis of the Federal Data Protection Act (BDSG). On the other hand there are also numerous new legal data protection requirements which must be fulfilled and complied with simply because of significantly increased sanctions and fines. Social pressure to protect the personal data of interested parties will increase in the future.

The new Federal Data Protection Act (BDSG-neu), alongside data protection laws of the federal states and other area-specific regulations, governs the handling of personal data of interested parties which are processed in information and communication systems or manually. It implements the Data Protection Directive which has been repealed and replaced by the General Data Protection Regulation. The new version of the BDSG came into force at the same time in 2018.

The objectives of the GDPR are the protection of the fundamental rights and freedoms of natural persons and in particular their right to protection of their personal data (Art. 1(2) GDPR) and the free movement of personal data (Art. 1(3) GDPR).

These objectives are to be achieved through the principles of personal data processing set out in Art. 5 GDPR: lawfulness, fairness, transparency, purpose limitation, data minimisation, accuracy, storage limitation, integrity and confidentiality, accountability. Also new and important is the right to erasure (right to be forgotten) of personal data combined with the corresponding evidence of implementation.

Table of overviews and comparisons

Designation	Author	Status	Focus	Assessment
CobiT	ISACA		Method for ensuring completeness of a control environment for quality, security and orderliness	
DIN 31644	DIN	Standard	Long-term digital archiving, mostly for libraries	Certification
GDPR	European Union	Regulation	General Data Protection Regulation for personal data	According to the Bavarian Data Protection Authority (BayLDA) certification will be supported by the authorities
EU Regulation 910/2014 (eIDAS)	European Union	Regulation	Electronic Identification, Authentication and Trust Services for electronic transactions (within the EU single market)	Certification
GoBD	BMF	Decree	Orderliness of commercial documents	No assessment as per decree
GoBS (replaced by GoBD as from 1.1.2015)	AWV/BMF	Decree	Orderliness of commercial documents	Attestation by a financial auditor
IDW ERS FAIT 1-3	IDW	Standard	Auditability for commercial documents	Attestation by a financial auditor
ISO 19600	DIN/ISO	Standard	Compliance management systems	Certification
ISO 27001	DIN/ISO	Standard	Information security management systems	Certification
ISO 27002	DIN/ISO	Standard	Information security management systems	Addition to ISO 27001
ISO 27017 & ISO 27018	DIN/ISO	Standard	Information security management systems	Addition to ISO 27001 – security and data protection in the cloud sector
ISO 9000	DIN/ISO	Standard	Quality management system for products	Certification
IT Grundschutz	BSI	Methodo-logy	Technical Information security	Certification (in combination with ISO 27001)
ITIL	Cabinet Office	Standard	Basis for the implementation of an IT Management System	Against ISO/IEC 20000-1
AC-DMS	VOI and TÜViT	Standard	General auditability for document management and document processes	Certification
TR 03125 (ESOR)	BSI	Technical Regulation	Long-term archiving whilst preserving value as evidence	Product certification
TR 03138 (RESISCAN)	BSI	Technical Regulation	Replacement scanning	Process certification
Vertrauens-dienste-gesetz (VDG)	Bund	Law	National addition to eIDAS regulation	Replaces Federal Signature Act

11.1.1. Assignment of content of the AC-DMS structure to ISO 27001

In order to make the relationship between various IT security and IT compliance procedures clear within an example, the following table shows a comparison between the AC-DMS structure and the structure of ISO/IEC 27001:2017:

11.1.2. Assignment of content of the AC-DMS structure to ISO/IEC 27001

DIN EN ISO/IEC 27001:2017		AC-DMS	
Group	Content	Criteria	Content
5	Information security policy	4, 10	IT security, Internal control system
6	Organisation of information security		
7	Human resource security	4	IT security
8	Asset management	1, 10	General description of the area of use, Internal control system
9	Access control	4	IT security
10	Cryptography		
11	Physical and environmental security	4, 5	IT security, Technical operation
12	Operations security		
13	Communications security	4	IT security
14	System acquisition, development and maintenance	5	Technical operation
15	Supplier relationships	9	Outsourcing
16	Information security incident management	4, 5	IT security, Technical operation
17	Information security aspects of business continuity management	5	Technical operation
18	Compliance	4, 10	IT security, Internal control system

AC-DMS		DIN EN ISO/IEC 27001:2017	
Criteria	Content	Group	Content
1	General description of the area of use	5	Information security policy
2	Task-related and inherently logical solution	8, 18	Asset management, Compliance
3	Technical solution	12, 13	Operations security, Communications security
4	IT security	5, 6, 7, 9, 10, 11, 12, 13	Information security policy, Organisation of information security, Human resource security, Access control, Cryptography, Physical and environmental security, Operations security, Communications security
5	Technical operation	11, 12, 14, 16	Physical and environmental security, Operations security, System acquisition, development and maintenance, Information security incident management
6	Long-term availability and migration	5, 6, 11, 17	Information security policy, Organisation of information security, Physical and environmental security, Information security aspects of business continuity management
7	Qualification of employees	7	Human resource security
8	Testing	5, 12, 14	Information security policy, Operations security, System acquisition, development and maintenance
9	Outsourcing	15	Supplier relationships
10	Description of the Internal Control System (ICS)	5, 16, 18	Information security policy, Information security incident management, Compliance